RUTH

ABINGDON OLD TESTAMENT COMMENTARIES

RUTH

JUDY FENTRESS-WILLIAMS

Abingdon Press
Nashville

ABINGDON OLD TESTAMENT COMMENTARIES
RUTH

Library of Congress Cataloging-in-Publication Data
Fentress-Williams, Judy.
  Ruth / Judy Fentress-Williams.
     pages   cm -- (Abingdon Old Testament commentaries)
  Includes bibliographical references.
  ISBN 978-1-4267-4625-3 (book - pbk. / trade pbk. : alk. paper)   1. Bible. O.T. Ruth—
Commentaries.   I. Title.
  BS1315.53.F46 2012
  222'.3507—dc23

                                                                    2012008655

12 13 14 15 16 17 18 19 20 21—10 9 8 7 6 5 4 3 2 1

MANUFACTURED IN THE UNITED STATES OF AMERICA

CONTENTS

CONTENTS

ACKNOWLEDGMENTS

This commentary is, among other things, about dialogue. Therefore, I am grateful for the conversation partners who have, through their dialogue with me, contributed to this book.

I am indebted to those conversation partners who listened and responded to my ideas about Ruth when they were no more than a few key words on a mind map scratched out on a paper napkin. They include Miriam Therese Winter, Donna Manocchio, Victoria Hoffer, Neff Powell, and Delbert Flowers. Thank you for being such patient and attentive midwives.

The classes I have been blessed to teach in a variety of settings have afforded me the opportunity to try out my ideas and receive much-needed feedback. In particular, I would like to thank the Alfred Street Baptist Church Bible Study and Christian Leadership Institute, the Chapel School classes at Howard University, the "Bad Girls in the Bible" class at the Evening School at Virginia Theological Seminary, the Women's Leadership Institute at Hartford Seminary, and All Saints' Episcopal Church in Austin, Texas, where I gave the Bailey Lectures in 2010.

I owe a debt of gratitude to Dean Ian Markham of Virginia Theological Seminary for his enthusiastic and unflagging support of this project, particularly through the establishment of the Meade Seminar for faculty research and writing. The Meade Seminar, administered by Dean of the Faculty Tim Sedgwick, provided an ongoing opportunity to work on this project with a community of scholars whose input and commentary inspired and sustained me. Thank you Stephen Cook, Kathy Grieb, Barney Hawkins, Lloyd Anthony Lewis, Ian Markham, Kate Sonderegger, and Kathy Staudt for reading those early drafts and modeling an ideal dialogic community.

Christine Falstich is to be thanked for her careful work on the subject index as is the staff of the Bishop Payne Library at Virginia Theological Seminary for their support of my research.

The conversations with the series editors, Kathleen O'Connor and Patrick Miller, were a blessing in every sense of the word. They were able to see the larger picture when I was lost in details and they kept me to task. Linda Lanam gave of her gifts and time to assist with editing the manuscript. Thank you.

Finally, I want to thank my husband, Kevin, and my children, Sam and Jacob, for reminding me on a daily basis in familiar and surprising ways that I have more than one vocation. I love you dearly and I am blessed to call you my own.

I would like to dedicate this book to Pearl and Gerri Flowers—a mother-in-law and daughter-in-law who are women of strength (*hayil*) and faithfulness (*hesed*).

FOREWORD

The *Abingdon Old Testament Commentaries* are offered to the reader in hopes that they will aid in the study of Scripture and provoke a deeper understanding of the Bible in all its many facets. The texts of the Old Testament come out of a time, a language, and socio-historical and religious circumstances far different from the present. Yet Jewish and Christian communities have held to them as a sacred canon, significant for faith and life in each new time. Only as one engages these books in depth and with all the critical and intellectual faculties available to us can the contemporary communities of faith and other interested readers continue to find them meaningful and instructive.

These volumes are designed and written to provide compact, critical commentaries on the books of the Old Testament for the use of theological students and pastors. It is hoped that they may be of service also to upper-level college or university students and to those responsible for teaching in congregational settings. In addition to providing basic information and insights into the Old Testament writings, these commentaries exemplify the tasks and procedures of careful interpretation.

The writers of the commentaries in this series come from a broad range of ecclesiastical affiliations, confessional stances, and educational backgrounds. They have experience as teachers and, in some instances, as pastors and preachers. In most cases, the authors are persons who have done significant research on the book that is their assignment. They take full account of the most important current scholarship and secondary literature, while not attempting to summarize that literature or to engage in technical academic debate. The fundamental concern of each volume is analysis and discussion of the literary, socio-historical, theological, and ethical dimensions of the biblical texts themselves.

The New Revised Standard Version of the Bible is the principal translation of reference for the series, though authors may draw upon other interpretations in their discussion. Each writer is attentive to the original Hebrew text in preparing the commentary. But the authors do not presuppose any knowledge of the biblical languages on the part of the reader. When some awareness of a grammatical, syntactical, or philological issue is necessary for an adequate understanding of a particular text, the issue is explained simply and concisely.

Each volume consists of four parts. An *introduction* looks at the book as a whole to identify *key issues* in the book, its *literary genre* and *structure,* the *occasion and situational context* of the book (including both social and historical contexts), and the *theological* and *ethical* significance of the book.

The *commentary* proper organizes the text by literary units and, insofar as is possible, divides the comment into three parts. The *literary analysis* serves to introduce the passage with particular attention to identification of the genre of speech or literature and the structure or outline of the literary unit under discussion. Here also the author takes up significant stylistic features to help the reader understand the mode of communication and its impact on comprehension and reception of the text. The largest part of the comment is usually found in the *exegetical analysis,* which considers the leading concepts of the unit, the language of expression, and problematical words, phrases, and ideas in order to get at the aim or intent of the literary unit, as far as that can be uncovered. Attention is given here to particular historical and social situations of the writer(s) and reader(s) where that is discernible and relevant as well as to wider cultural (including religious) contexts. The analysis does not proceed phrase by phrase or verse by verse but deals with the various particulars in a way that keeps in view the overall structure and central focus of the passage and its relationship to the general line of thought or rhetorical argument of the book as a whole. The final section, *theological and ethical analysis,* seeks to identify and clarify the theological and ethical matters with which the unit deals or to which it points. Though not aimed primarily at contemporary issues of faith and life, this section should provide readers a basis for reflection on them.

Each volume also contains a select bibliography of works cited in the commentary as well as major commentaries and other important works available in English.

The fundamental aim of this series will have been attained if readers are assisted not only in understanding more about the origins, character, and meaning of the Old Testament writings but also in entering into their own informed and critical engagement with the texts themselves.

Patrick D. Miller
General Editor

INTRODUCTION

D escribed by Goethe as "the most charming little whole" of antiquity, Ruth has long been recognized for its literary quality (Dunker, 217). This beautifully composed narrative continues to attract readers across generations and boundaries of gender, class, and ethnicity. In fact, the beauty of the book often distracts from the practical nature of the narrative. For all of its appeal, Ruth is, after all, a story about family and survival. The marriage between Ruth and Boaz is a levirate marriage. The goal of this practice is to ensure the continuation and stability of the family line. Thus this "charming little whole" has as its subject preservation of life in the face of death and upholding memory to ward off the loss of identity.

This story of survival is short; it consists of four chapters with elements of loss and recovery, famine and harvest, barrenness and fruitfulness, life and death. These elements afford the book a broad appeal as it speaks to various stages and seasons of life, all the while upholding the power of faithfulness against an ever-changing backdrop. Named after one of the major characters, the book of Ruth tells the story of Naomi of Bethlehem and her family "in the days when the judges ruled" (Ruth 1:1).

The story is summarized as follows: Naomi, her husband, Elimelech, and their two sons leave their home in Bethlehem and sojourn to Moab during a famine. While there, Elimelech dies. The two sons, Mahlon and Chilion, take Moabite wives and then after a period of time Mahlon and Chilion die as well, leaving the women widowed and childless. Naomi receives word that there is food in Bethlehem, and she begins to return with her daughters-in-law. On the way to Bethlehem, Naomi stops and urges the young widows to return to their own homes so they could have a chance at marriage. They both resist, but after Naomi's insistence, Orpah eventually and reluctantly returns home. Ruth refuses to leave Naomi and accompanies her to Bethlehem at the time of harvest. To provide sustenance for herself and her mother-in-law, Ruth gleans in the fields and draws the attention of the landowner Boaz (a relative of Naomi), who is kind to her and allows her to glean in his fields with preferential treatment. At the end of the harvest, Naomi develops a plan to secure their future. Ruth goes along with the plan, which involves going to Boaz on the threshing floor under the cover of darkness, uncovering his feet, and asking for Boaz's protection. Boaz praises Ruth for her faithfulness and agrees to take care of her. At the story's end, Boaz secures the right as kinsman/redeemer and marries Ruth. Ruth and Boaz have a son named Obed, who becomes the grandfather of David, king of Israel.

Literary Aspects

A Text in Dialogue

Ruth begins "in the days that the judges ruled," and ends with a genealogy that includes King David. These temporal bookends of Ruth make intentional connections to the surrounding material in Judges, Samuel, and Kings. The Bible's proclivity to make connections with other narratives I will call dialogue. Ruth engages in dialogue with a number of texts. One obvious connection is the aforementioned opening and closing references. In addition, the book of Ruth contains explicit references to Rachel, Leah, and Tamar, all matriarchs of Genesis (Ruth 4:11-12), which allows the story to reach far back to the traditions of the ancestors. There are also implicit, structural references to Lot and his daughters in chapter 3, which will be explored later. Hence, in Ruth we observe the various strands of the text interacting with one another to form a dialogue.

The motifs and patterns in Ruth are laden with an acute awareness of the past. Elimelech moves his family because of famine, but moving for food is nothing new. The migration of a family because of famine is a contextual reality and an established pattern in Old Testament texts (Abraham in Gen 12:10; Isaac in Gen 26:1; and Jacob in Gen 46). Naomi and Ruth's daring plan to preserve the family follows the motif of the woman who goes to extremes to preserve the family line like Tamar in Gen 38. This results in a narrative that is aware of other stories and the way they are told. It makes use of established patterns to connect the Ruth narrative to others.

The narrative engages other moments in Israel's overarching salvation history. Every word then carries a multitude of possible meanings, and perception or understanding is affected by the presence of another. This creates expectations in the reader that meaning in the narrative will come from the multiple voices in the text and that there is the ongoing possibility of new meanings. The theologies and perspectives that produce the various strands in conversation form a meaning that is larger than any single voice or perspective.

Thus reading the Bible is much like reading music that is written in parts. Just as the reader of such music may focus her eye on one part, she is aware that there is more to the song—she is free to look at the notes above and below, and see how each part contributes to a fuller, richer composition. Similarly, since the language of Scripture is inherently dialogic, the reader understands that any one part in isolation is limited in its ability to realize its fullness of meaning. Each written and spoken word exists for the purpose of working toward meaning in dialogue with other words, which means there is always some new meaning to be found in the text.

The analogy of a text with music in parts, like all analogies, has its limits. Most music written in parts is harmonious. Most moments of disharmony are eventually resolved. Although we may look for and expect a harmonious dialogue in Scripture, there is no guarantee that will always be the case. Moreover, in music, there is a designated location for the various parts. Again,

Scripture is not so orderly. The references in Scripture reach forward and backward, connecting narratives by patterns, functions, names, events, locations, phrases, blessings, and so forth. There is no set pattern for references, which means the dialogues between them can happen in many ways. It is also to be noted that the references to other narratives only work if the reader is aware of the other narratives. For example, the fact that the genealogy of Ruth ends with David is significant only to those readers who know that David is the beloved king of Israel, the man after God's own heart, with whom God made an eternal covenant. Finally the dialogue of Scripture is ongoing. The stories of Scripture reach out and invite new readers to enter the conversation and become a part of the story. This means that in Scripture the story is never completed—with the presence of dialogue there is always the hope of additional meaning (Morson and Emerson 1990, 37).

Not only is the book of Ruth open to dialogue with a variety of texts, it consists primarily of dialogue. Fifty-five of the eighty-eight verses are dialogue—speeches and conversations among or by the characters. These dialogues among the characters affirm, shape, and assert an identity that would not exist otherwise. The characters use language to describe their location in relationship to one another. Moreover, the exchanges among characters reveal a truth greater than any individual can comprehend. The dialogues direct and surprise the reader, exposing the limits of social and cultural constraints.

Genre

When we assign a genre to a text, we are not so much defining a text as we are describing it based on the characteristics observed by the interpreter. For the book of Ruth, there is general consensus that the text is narrative prose. Beyond that basic designation, Ruth has been further classified as a novella, a folktale, and comedy. Each of these definitions provides the reader with a clue as to how the interpreter reads the text.

The designation of Ruth as a folktale makes a claim that the structure, roles of characters, and function of the narrative are the primary characteristics of the story. Since the folktale is a form that is self-contained, historical background is not essential to understanding the story (Sasson 1979, 216).

Like the folktale, the designation of Ruth as novella is primarily based upon literary qualities. Ruth is often classified as a novella because it has a clear, self-contained plot and it makes intentional use of literary devices. First, a novella has a distinct literary style that contains poetic elements found in direct speech. Second, the characters in novellas are often ordinary people who find themselves in extraordinary circumstances. Third, novellas are both entertaining and instructive (Campbell 1975, 5). All three of these defining characteristics apply to Ruth.

The designations of folktale and novella have implications for the historicity of the text. Scholars deem some genres as "ahistorical" in nature. A short story, for example, by definition need not make a historical claim. Similarly, a "novella" is characterized by the development of characters in the story and not by the presence of fact. Thus with the designation of short story or novella we are asserting that the "truths" of the narrative reside in the structure, function, or literary artistry and not the historical accuracy of the account. This is not to suggest that Ruth is not historical. It is clearly placed in "the days when the judges ruled," premonarchical Israel (1200–1020 BCE). However, "novella" asserts that history is in service to the narrative and not the other way around. The story is placed in a specific time, but it is not limited to a singular temporal perspective.

Like the novella, a comedy has a distinct literary style that subjects characters to extraordinary circumstances, and it is entertaining and instructive. Moreover, the comedy has a structure that begins in harmony, moves into chaos, and usually moves toward a happy ending that satisfies the audience (Frye 1957, 167). This movement from harmony to chaos and then to resolution is tied to the shift in location. In comedy, the change in setting is often the way that movement from one social center to another is achieved and relocation creates a crisis in identity. The shift in location results in obstacles for the characters and the work of the comedy is to move the characters forward on the scenes of discovery and reconciliation. Agricultural cultures usually have a comedy-like drama that is associated with harvest or the change in seasons (Johnston, 7).

In offering an alternate reality with its own rules, a comedy is poised to provide commentary or critique on the customs, mores, and rules of a given society, all the while entertaining its audience. In a comedy the established rules of a community are the illusion, and reality is the antithesis of that illusion. In other words, comedy pushes against the restrictive nature of society with a new set of rules that challenges the status quo (Frye 1957, 163). Thus a comedy has as its goal both the transformation of the characters and that of the audience.

Using a comedic structure, the book of Ruth introduces an alternate reality—a Moabite woman who demonstrates faithfulness (*hesed*) that transforms the existing reality. Ruth's faithfulness allows her to escape the role of foreigner/outsider to which she is proscribed by cultural mores. Her transition from "incestuous bastard" (Bailey 1995, 128) to revered ancestress gives Israel a new lens through which to view those outside the people of God. Since much of this transformation results from dialogue between the characters in the story and the dialogue between the reader and the text, I will read Ruth as a dialogic comedy.

If we read Ruth through a comedic lens we understand that part of its function is to challenge the established reality of the culture that reads it. When we describe Ruth as a dialogic comedy, the challenge comes through the dialogue in and between texts; its function to challenge the status quo is an ongoing one. In other words, Ruth has the potential to challenge early and late, ancient and modern communities.

Structure

The structure of Ruth, along with the literary artistry, contributes to the long-standing appeal of the book. The internal structure of each chapter is similar. Each of the four chapters contains three sections and dialogue is at the center of each chapter. This dialogue is about identity. In chapter 1 Ruth claims an identity. In chapter 2 Boaz assigns a title to Ruth that designates her as family. In chapter 3 Ruth asks Boaz to marry her, thus altering her identity, and in chapter 4 the narrative genealogy and the concluding genealogy challenges the very construct of identity.

When we examine the external structure, we observe a relationship between chapters 1 and 4 and between chapters 2 and 3 based on content and setting/location. The famine and death in chapter 1 is resolved by life and harvest in chapter 4. Chapters 2 and 3 are in temporal opposition to each other. Chapter 2 takes place during the day when Ruth gleans to procure food, and chapter 3 takes place at night when Naomi sends Ruth to the threshing floor.

Another pattern becomes evident when we examine the narrative use of location in Ruth. The locations of the central or main action in chapters 1 and 3 are mysterious, liminal, and possibly even supernatural. For example, Ruth binds herself to Naomi somewhere between Moab and Bethlehem, in an undisclosed location. Ruth asks Boaz to be her redeemer on the threshing floor at night, when there is no one to witness the encounter. Both events are outside the realm of normal, public activity. In contrast, the central narrative action in chapters 2 and 4 are in public places, where witnesses and formal language abound. Boaz has an exchange with Ruth in his field in the day, presumably surrounded by his supervisors and perhaps other workers. In chapter 4 he conducts business with his relative in a public space, the city gate, in the presence of elders that he has assembled. Thus the action of the narrative takes place in two realms—the public, official one, and the secret, unofficial realm, where the lack of witnesses and/or daylight in chapter 3 keeps these events cloaked in mystery.

Placement

The book of Ruth has occupied more than one spot in the canon of Scripture. Hebrew Scripture divides into three sections, *Torah* (teaching, law), *Nevi'im* (prophets), and *Ketuvim* (writings). Ruth belongs to the third division of Hebrew Scripture, which was canonized after the first two, and represents a broad span of time and a variety of genres. Within *Ketuvim,* Ruth appears in a collection called the *Megilloth,* or festival scrolls, along with Lamentations, Esther, Song of Songs, and Ecclesiastes. If the *Megilloth* is ordered according to presumed date of authorship, Ruth occupies the first position. With this ordering, the book of Ruth follows the book of Proverbs. In this context, the story of Ruth comes on the heels of the virtuous woman described in Proverbs 31 and Ruth can be seen as an example of this virtuous woman. Here the term translated as virtuous is *"hayil,"* connoting strength. *Hayil* is usually used to describe physical strength in men. That it is applied to a woman in Proverbs 31 and then to Ruth (Ruth 3:11), offers a richer understanding of strength.

Some order the *Megilloth* based on when they are read liturgically, which begin with the spring of each new year. When this happens, Ruth is the second in the collection. This ordering begins with Song of Songs, which is associated with Passover, followed by Ruth on Shavuot or the Feast of Weeks (May–June), Lamentations on the ninth of Av/the commemoration of the destruction of the Temple (July–August), Ecclesiastes/Qohelet on Sukkot or the Feast of Tabernacles (September–October), and Esther on Purim (March). In this ordering, Ruth, a story of famine and harvest, follows a song of longing and desire.

The Septuagint, the Greek translation of the Old Testament, places Ruth after the book of Judges, strengthening its connection to the Davidic monarchy. The book begins "in the days that the Judges ruled" (Ruth 1:1), and ends with the words "and Jesse [the father] of David" (Ruth 4:22). This is the placement that makes its way into the Christian tradition because the ordering of the books in the Septuagint eventually becomes the ordering of the books in most English translations of the Bible. Thus Christian communities have encountered Ruth earlier in the Old Testament, in the section of the Bible following the Torah/Pentateuch that some call the former prophets. The placement of Ruth between Judges and Samuel allows the book to fit in the narrative time line between tribal rulers and the monarchy.

Each of these locations within Scripture offers a different conversation partner for the book of Ruth. On the one hand, the genealogy and references to the period of the judges place it in

Israel's chronology. On the other hand, the literary artistry of the narrative makes the historical characters metaphorical, enabling them to transcend time. This little book is well suited to these multiple conversations and is able to function in more than one literary context. Even though Ruth is placed in a specific time, the events of famine and harvest are not limited to one time period. Nor are the themes of loss and recovery, death and birth. The presence of these themes allows Ruth to be in and beyond time.

Dating

One of the benefits of assigning a date to a text is that it sheds light on the context of the writers and earliest audiences that can provide the reader with a lens to interpret what we encounter. Having a general sense of when Ruth was written may provide the reader with a specific political climate, approximate historical events, and context for customs and practices that could assist in the reading of the text. For all the benefits that dating a text may offer, this is not easily achieved with the book of Ruth. For the most part, scholars occupy two positions on the date of composition; early (around the time of King David, ninth century BCE) and late (the early postexilic period, sixth–fifth centuries BCE). The arguments for these dates are based on language and content, and from those details come suggestions about the cultural/historical context.

Scholars who support a later date, sixth–fifth century BCE, notice the presence of Aramaisms, namely linguistic features such as vocabulary and syntax that represent a later form of biblical Hebrew. The text's explanation of the sandal ceremony in Ruth 4:7 ("Now this was the custom in former times in Israel concerning redeeming and exchanging: to confirm a transaction, one party took off a sandal and gave it to the other; this was the manner of attesting in Israel.") supports the argument that this is a later text telling a story about an earlier time to an audience who needs to have earlier practices explained.

The scholars who subscribe to a later date argue that the migratory elements of the book speak to the experience of exile and return to the land. Some argue that the book of Ruth was a contemporary of Ezra and Nehemiah. As such, Ruth can be seen as a response to the passages in Ezra that recount the sending away of foreign wives and children upon return to the promised land. In Ezra, the Israelites are allowed to return from exile by the decree of King Cyrus of Persia. After the Temple was rebuilt, the priest Ezra arrives and the people confess their sin in marrying foreign women (Ezra 9:1-4). Ezra prays for the people who subsequently decide to make a covenant with God, "to send away all these wives and their children" (Ezra 10:3).

If Ruth was written at the time of Ezra, the story includes a covenant in chapter 1 that binds a foreign wife to a prominent house in Bethlehem of Judah. This foreign woman is a symbol of faithfulness and strength.

In more recent years, the scholarly consensus has shifted from assigning Ruth to the postexilic period to the time of the Davidic monarchy. In spite of the Aramaisms, the language of Ruth is described as classical, which would support the argument for an earlier date of composition. Those arguing for the earlier date of the ninth century BCE suggest that David's Moabite ancestry would have been a point of contention in Israel, and the Ruth narrative would have been an apology for Ruth and David. This position contends that the references to David in Ruth are strategic and cannot be ignored. Had the narrative been written later, David's dynasty would not have needed defending because by the sixth— fifth century BCE, the line of David was (unequivocally) revered. However, David may have been in need of defense while he was on the throne. His reign could have been challenged by supporters of the house of Saul. It is also possible that David's dynasty would have been challenged when his son Solomon became king.

As these arguments show, the evidence used to make the case for an early or late composition date is not definitive. Linguistic evidence has been interpreted to support earlier and later dates, and the cultural/historical arguments made in support of a later composition date, sixth—fifth century, are no weaker or stronger than the argument for an earlier date, ninth century.

Another challenge to the process of dating a text is the oral tradition. It is quite possible that the story of Ruth existed during the reign of David in oral form and could not be written at that time as an official document. It was only later, after the Davidic monarchy ended, that the story could be told. An example from American history is useful here. It is now widely acknowledged and accepted that the third president of the United States, Thomas Jefferson, had a relationship with his slave Sally Hemings, and that this relationship resulted in children. The president's relationship with Sally Hemings could not be openly acknowledged or discussed during his presidency, but it is also the case that a number of people knew about it. Generations had to pass before the story could be acknowledged. The unofficial history can only become a part of the official story when the keepers of the tradition feel it is safe to do so.

Ultimately, one of the strengths of Ruth, its compatible dialogue with a number of texts, is the very same quality that contributes to the difficulty of dating the text based on content. If the reader understands Ruth as a counterargument to the polemic of Ezra–Nehemiah, it could be assigned a later date. If it is written to legitimize the Davidic monarchy and the rightful place of Moab within the borders of Israel when Solomon's status was in jeopardy, it could be assigned an earlier date. There is no disadvantage to assigning the earlier date to Ruth, because it means the story had influence in earlier and later generations. The assignment of an earlier date (the Davidic monarchy) does not exclude the possibility that Ruth was retold as a response to Ezra–Nehemiah.

Tradition and Countertradition

The parts of Scripture that become tradition are often those elements that reflect and support the values of the culture that preserves them. In some instances the narrative can shape the values of the community that receives them. For example, the cultures that provide a foundation for the Old Testament are patriarchal ones. It then follows that the majority of fully developed characters are men. It stands to reason that women in the narrative are cast in supportive roles, serving as background or as a foil to their male counterparts. In Ruth, we observe an alternative model where the women exist in the foreground. This alternative model is a countertradition that stands alongside these mainstream characterizations and worldviews. In Scripture there are not only the expected traditions or "official" voices but there are also the countertraditions or "unofficial" voices.

For example, the story of the exodus contains traditions centered on the prophet Moses, and it would be rare to find an account of the exodus that fails to mention him. The first story of deliverance in the book of Exodus is that of the midwives in chapter 1, yet many retellings of the exodus omit this tradition. The subplots that exist and operate on the periphery of the community's collective memory are countertradition. They often reflect the cultural contexts and values of the communities that retell the stories.

Because we are accustomed to reading in such a way that the climax of a story (particularly one with a comedic structure) comes at the end, our tradition trains us to look for this major moment of the narrative at the end and in the resolution. For many readers of Ruth, this results in a reading that sees the genealogy that includes David as the climax of the story. A countertraditional reading focuses on the power of Ruth's vow to Naomi at the beginning of the narrative. It is the moment that gives birth to the rest of the narrative; it is a creation of a new understanding of family that is based not just on blood, but in faithfulness (*hesed*). It is Ruth's vow, her "action speech," that allows for the rest of the narrative action to occur.

As such, the vow that takes place between two relatively unknown women in an unknown place offers an alternative to a narrow definition of family rooted in patriarchy. It is the opening and decisive action in the narrative. As such, the vow forms the center of the narrative. Now we come to understand the relationship between tradition and countertradition differently. It is not the case that countertradition exists quietly alongside the traditions. Rather, in Ruth, the tradition is born out of the countertradition. Tradition is an outward or public manifestation of something that has already occurred in the margins.

Themes in Ruth

Identity

A number of themes have been identified in Ruth, including those of marriage (levirate marriage, marriage with foreigners); women (prominence of women, gender roles); and survival, love, harvest, covenant, and faithfulness (*hesed*). An often overlooked theme of the book is that of identity. This commentary will use identity as a primary lens for interpretation. I define identity as the set of characteristics that allows a person to be known and identified within a group. These characteristics and values assigned by any given community come out of the life of that community and serve its interests. In other words, identity is a construct formed by cultures that serves a purpose. Identity determines who is an insider and who is an outsider. How and why the category of "other" is defined and used in a culture will indicate the values and mores that are important to a community at a given time. Moreover, the aspects of identity that do not fit easily into the construct or defy the existing construct will point out what issues a community is struggling with at a given time.

In much of the ancient Near Eastern (ANE) world, as in many contemporary cultures (African, Asian, Latino, etc.), family was the center of identity and survival. The well-known phrase, "I am because we are," aptly conveys a sense of self that was tied to the family group. The goal of the family was to thrive (be sustained and grow), which required health (adequate nutrition and longevity), a sustaining environment, and procreation, and ultimately the avoidance of death. The danger of death was far more than one's removal from the earth. It was the removal of one's name and memory from the earth—the loss of one's name and the loss of memory was to be avoided at all costs. Family defended against this terrible fate. The descendants were trained to remember those who went before—just as many contemporary Jewish families maintain a practice of naming a newborn for a deceased ancestor—in so doing the name and memory of the deceased is maintained. In the book of Ruth we observe that ancient Israel had a family-based, lineage-based culture. Identity was inextricably tied to the family, and the family name (reputation and memory).

Family, in turn, was associated with a particular land or location. The nuclear families and extended families (kinship groups and tribes) were affiliated with a particular geographic region (not unlike the way some southern families are associated with a particular area, i.e., the Joneses of Suffolk County). The family members lived, died, and were buried on their land and the land was passed down from one generation to the next. Burial practices reflect a worldview where the family's well-being, even its very existence, was tied to the family plot. For this reason, association with the land was important in death as well as life. Deceased members of the family were buried in the family tomb. This practice of being "gathered unto the fathers" assured the remembrance of the deceased even after life. The deceased were physically present with the family and on the land of the family and that presence supported the memory of the deceased among the living relatives. The memory of the deceased protected against death. In other words, so long as the deceased were remembered by the remaining family members they were still "alive."

Death was not final. The lack of memory or the possibility of being buried away from the family was the fate to be avoided at all costs. One did not want to be "cut off" from the land or from the family. Each time a family group (Elimelech and his family in chapter 1) or individuals (Ruth and Orpah) move away from home, they risk a serious threat to their identity. Ruth, for example, upon moving from Moab to Bethlehem becomes "the Moabite" whereas she was not so identified in the land of Moab. Thus the shift in location has an impact on her identity. In Moab, calling her a "Moabite" would have been redundant. In Moab, Ruth was an insider. It is only when she leaves her homeland, where her identity was understood, and migrates to Bethlehem that she becomes "other," and vulnerable.

Identity based on a family-linage-land model was not unique to Israel. A number of her neighbors honored similar if not identical practices when it came to connection to land and family. However, Israel's identity was formed over and against these other groups. One can trace through Israel's history a struggle to maintain a sense of identity over against those who surround her. The father of Israel, Abraham, was called to leave his father, his father's house, and land to forge a new people, a separate identity. The irony of the Abraham icon, of course, is that he eventually comes to be associated with three religions, Judaism, Christianity, and Islam. Embedded in the story of Israel is a struggle to form an identity in opposition to her "relatives" that surrounded her. This identity is grounded in the exclusive worship of YHWH, but because of Israel's geographic, cultural, and ethnic proximity to those who surround her, that identity is carefully guarded. It is for this reason that the language used to warn about the other is so vehement. Those who used to be family become other in the attempt to uphold a construct of identity as a people set apart.

Here the issue of dating takes on added significance. If Ruth was written during the reign of David, it serves to defend the king and legitimize his Moabite roots. One date, that of the Davidic monarchy, would seek to make David legitimate within the existing framework of identity, positing Ruth as an exception to the ban. The later date of Ruth, which would form a dialogue with Ezra–Nehemiah, goes further in that it challenges the legitimacy of the ban against the Moabites in that time. In other words, it asks, will God turn his face away forever? Is mercy intended only for Israel?

Each chapter in the book of Ruth contains the elements of location, dialogue, and identity and as such, each chapter engages in a dialogue about location and identity. In each chapter there is a central action, a decisive moment or act in the chapter that determines how the narrative will move forward. Each of these moments involves an encounter of sorts. Ruth is involved in each of the encounters that are turning points. In chapter 1, Ruth makes a vow to Naomi in an undisclosed location between Moab and Judah. By making this vow, Ruth pledges her life and her identity to Naomi and her family. In chapter 2, Boaz invites Ruth into a dialogue and then a meal at his field calling her, "my daughter" pointing to a shift in identity. The third chapter's encounter involves Ruth and Boaz on the threshing floor. There she asks him for his protection, which would lead to another shift in identity. In the final chapter, where Ruth has no spoken words, she marries Boaz. No specific location for the wedding is given here, but we presume it occurred in a marriage chamber.

Encounters among characters operate on multiple levels. On a literary level, the encounter is a device that moves the narrative forward. For example, Naomi and Ruth have an identity crisis in chapter 1. The movement toward Bethlehem stops as Naomi realizes she cannot go home with her Moabite daughters-in-law. The encounter between Naomi and Ruth in chapter 1 results in a covenant that redefines their identities. Ruth binds herself to Naomi, her people, and her God. Now the women can continue on to Bethlehem. The covenant invites God into the identity crisis that allows their relationship and the narrative to move beyond the impasse of their differences. When God enters the story, none of the existing rules or conventions hold; we must be prepared for anything. A theological reading of the text will look for the presence of the divine in each encounter.

Identity, Ethnicity, and Gender

The story of Ruth takes place in a cultural context which, like all contexts, assigns value to gender and ethnicity. In this particular context, Ruth's gender and ethnicity limit her options. Like men, women in the ANE were assigned to specific roles within the family. Their names, sustenance, status, and fates came to them through the men in their lives, whether that was through their fathers, husbands, or sons. Women needed to "belong" to a man in a familial sense in order to have a recognized place in society. For this reason, it is easy to see why a woman who was childless or a widow had more to contend with than the loss of a loved one. The state of either widowhood or childlessness, or both, meant loss of income, status, and property. Such a woman suffered a loss of identity and had limited options. She was the embodiment of famine.

The story of Israel is one of formation of a people out of other peoples, so ethnicity weighs heavily in the construction of identity in this narrative. Ruth's ethnicity as a Moabite places her with a people who have a complicated history with Israel. Moab and Ammon are the sons of Abraham's nephew Lot by his two daughters who are born through a shameful act of incest (Gen 19:30-38). As descendants of Lot, the Moabites and Ammonites are related to Israel, descendants of Abraham. In the story of Israel's formation we observe how Moab becomes "other" or foreigner.

In addition to Moab's shameful origins, Num 22–24 recounts the story of Balaam, a prophet of Moab who not only refuses hospitality to Israel on their sojourn in the wilderness, but tries to curse them. Deuteronomy 23:4 recalls this past, and for that reason Moab could not be admitted to the "assembly of the LORD. Even to the tenth generation" (Deut 23:3). The prohibition goes further to say, "You shall never promote their welfare of their prosperity as long as you live" (Deut 23:6).

Historically, the Moabites are not harmless outsiders; they are a threat to core practices of Israel, that is, the worship of YHWH alone. They are associated with forbidden worship practices. God severely punished the people for intermarriage with Moabite women that resulted in the worship of false gods (Num 25). Later in the historical material, Solomon's love for foreign women is listed as his sin that resulted in him building "a high place for Chemosh the abomination of Moab" (1 Kgs 11:7). Later still in the prophetic materials, Moab is named as a place that will experience God's judgment (Isaiah, Jeremiah, Amos, Zephaniah).

The presence of Moab in the midst of Israel is a threat to Israel's well-being and very existence. However, in the story of Ruth, there is a reversal. Here, the presence of a Moabitess allows for new life. The existence of Ruth in the canon of sacred Scripture is a "shout-out" to the outliers of any society. Ruth is a countertradition that has become tradition. Thus our familiarity with this story should never undermine our wonder at its very presence in the Bible.

Identity and Levirate Marriage

A commentary on the book of Ruth must address levirate marriage. The resolution of the story comes when Boaz "redeems" the name of his kinsman Mahlon, and in so doing makes

Mahlon's widow (Ruth) his wife. This act is known as levirate marriage. Levirate marriage comes from the Latin term *levir* for a husband's brother, and describes the practice of substitute marriage that occurred and continues to take place in some cultures where a male heir must be present for the purpose of inheritance. If a woman is widowed and has no son, she has no right of inheritance since the goods are passed down from men to men. The practice of levirate marriage allows for the woman to be "married" to the next living male relative for the purpose of having a son. If a son is born of this union, he stands in for his father and receives his father's inheritance, which provides for the entire family. The practice of levirate marriage reminds the reader that the book of Ruth is the product of a culture in which men are the essential and vital members of the family. To put it plainly, every family must have a male head of household. Men own property and men provide, so marriage—even levirate marriage—in these contexts is a very practical decision made to support the extended family.

The story of Tamar and Judah in Genesis 38 provides another narrative example of levirate marriage (Gen 38). This story is thematically connected to Ruth. Levirate marriage is one of the connecting themes between these stories, along with questions around identity and foreign women. Tamar's first husband, Er, died, and his brother Onan was to act as the *levir*. He failed in his task and was killed. Tamar was asked to wait for the third brother, but in this narrative, that did not happen. Judah unwittingly becomes the *levir* in this narrative, which we will examine in greater depth in chapters 3 and 4.

Gleaning and "the Other"

Like levirate marriage, gleaning is another unfamiliar practice found in Ruth that needs to be explained. The legal corpora of Leviticus and Deuteronomy give instructions to provide for the poor, the widow, and the orphan, the disenfranchised of the community. The command to leave some of the harvest for those who have no means of support is a part of the Holiness Code in Lev

19:10. "You shall not strip your vineyard bare, or gather the fallen grapes of your vineyard; you shall leave them for the poor and the alien: I am the LORD your God." The instruction for gleaning in Deut 24:21-22, gives a rationale: "When you gather the grapes of your vineyard, do not glean what is left; it shall be for the alien, the orphan, and the widow. Remember that you were a slave in the land of Egypt; therefore I am commanding you to do this." Gleaning is a practice that Israel keeps because she remembers her own past as an alien and a slave, and because she remembers who God is. God has been faithful to Israel and Israel by extension demonstrates faithfulness to others by providing for those in need. Yahwism demands that one honor God by acknowledging the outsider.

On a cultural level, gleaning is associated with a particular subset of society. In our society, paying for groceries with public assistance (such as food stamps, WIC), working as a migrant laborer, or receiving welfare benefits are practices that are associated with, but not limited to, those who are brown, black, non-English-speaking, and single with children. Thus as we read the story of Ruth, we should consider the possibility that many of the people that she encountered would have viewed her with disdain because she was a gleaner.

The practice of gleaning in the story of Ruth, like marriage, is more than an anthropological or sociological occurrence. In this narrative the practices of levirate marriage, gleaning, famine, and harvest also serve as symbols and metaphors that are heavy with theological meaning. They connote salvaging, salvation, redemption, restoration, new life, and hope. This is one of the reasons Ruth has continuing appeal.

Theological Concerns

If the literary genre of comedy by definition challenges the societal status quo, a theological corollary results in the book of Ruth. This narrative about God and God's people challenges Israel's theology of identity. On the one hand, Israel's relationship with God is rooted in a sense of being called, chosen, and set apart from the other nations. The nation's integrity is tied to its ability to remain separate from other nations and be faithful to God. On the other hand, the resolution of the Ruth story depends on the integration of a Moabite woman. Ruth is a surprising heroine because she is the embodiment of all that threatens Israel's integrity. She represents what Israel has been conditioned to revile and fear.

The narrative about Ruth—her presence, her faithfulness, and her marriage into a prominent family that includes King David—violates several traditions upon which Israel's identity as a holy nation is built. The historical narrative makes links to other narratives (like that of Tamar in Gen 38), and thereby invites the hearers into a conversation around the theology of identity. I will identify three theological concerns:

1. Who is included in the family of God? Is our identity as God's children determined by whom we exclude or whom we include?
2. To what extent is identity affected by location? Specifically, how can Israel be the people of God in exile?
3. Does time have an impact on identity? In other words, how do subsequent generations interpret a received tradition?

First, whether Ruth's earliest audience is ca. ninth century BCE or sixth–fifth century BCE, both audiences would have been wrestling with this question of identity. Israel's originates from God's call to Abraham to "come out" from among his people and take on a new identity as God's own. On the one hand, the message is clear—Israel is to remain racially pure and intermarriage is forbidden—except when it is not. The story of Ruth is both expected and a surprise. Ruth is not the first foreigner to have a role in Israel's story. Ruth's story, along with other narratives about a foreigner who becomes a part of the family (Rahab, Tamar), raises a larger question: what is it about the person Ruth that overrides the very strong ban against Moab in Deuteronomy? Under what circumstances is the ban on marriage to foreign women lifted? Finally, is this story just about Ruth, or is it about foreign wives, asserting that God is never limited in whom God chooses to work through? Is it casting the net wider? Namely, does Ruth's marriage to Boaz describe the gathering in of people who used to be Israel's kin but are no longer? In contemporary terms the question for communities of faith is, will our identity be shaped by exclusion or inclusion? When is it unacceptable to include the other? What is the difference between welcoming and tolerating?

Second, Israel's identity was rooted not only in a sense of being chosen by God, but by a connection to a specific place: the land promised to the patriarch, Abraham. In that land, the Temple, the center of worship, is built. The narrative of Ruth involves Naomi's movement from home and a sense of self tied to a foreign land, and back again. The exile and deportation were the end of the Temple and so much of the religious practice that was core to identity. Ultimately, what does God require of a people who no longer have a homeland or temple? When the core practices are no longer accessible, what are the core values? Moreover, if the elements that constituted an identity construct are missing, how does any Israelite determine who they are? Can Israel be the people of God away from the land?

Third, God's promise to Abraham included numerous descendants. These subsequent generations are to be instructed in the "commandment—the statutes and the ordinances" (Deut 6:1) that God gave to the people through Moses. How do subsequent generations interpret a received tradition? For example, the book of Deuteronomy contains the provision for gleaning and the ban against the Moabites. How does Israel determine how to honor and uphold a received tradition over time? Who decides that the practice of gleaning is maintained but exceptions will be made to the ban on exogamy? How do we discern between what is tradition and what is countertradition? When and to what extent do we allow the voices on the margins of our past (and present) to influence and shape the communal identity?

In many ways, the genre of comedy and the presence of countertraditions in the narrative will provide the key to navigating the theological questions. A comedy expects a certain amount of flexibility of its readers—locations shift rapidly and characters are lost and found again; time lines and geography bend to accommodate the story. With a comedy, the readers are willing to suspend disbelief, because they know how comedy works; they trust that the genre will go to great lengths to bring them safely to the other side. Similarly, God's people need to be able to suspend preconceived notions and allow God to do the work that God intends to do. The theological equivalent of reading a comedy is facing any circumstance with a belief in a God who is able to work in any of our circumstances and make things right.

So much of what happens in Ruth happens where no one can see. Ruth binds herself to Naomi in the "in-between place" of Moab and Judah. No one is there to witness it. Similarly, Ruth asks Boaz for redemption in the middle of the night when we presume everyone else is asleep. These events allow for the inclusion of Ruth as Boaz's people, first as a gleaner and then as a wife. The pattern of what happens away from our observation and then bursts forth where we can see it draws on the images of planting and harvest, conception and birth. On a theological level, it suggests that in the famine times, God is planting seed, preparing for the next harvest, even when we cannot see it. We must conclude then that whatever we know or recognize about the work of God is only a small piece of the larger whole. We cannot know it all.

CHAPTER 1
A DIALOGUE OF DETERMINATION

Where you go, I will go;

where you lodge, I will lodge;

your people shall be my people,

and your God my God (Ruth 1:16b)

With these words, Ruth the Moabite states her intention to stay with Naomi her mother-in-law, even as Naomi tries to send her away. There is something unfathomable about Ruth's pledge. It is unexpected and lacks reasonable motivation. Her words reflect an undeterred faithfulness that stands out against their dire circumstances of barrenness and widowhood. That is why Ruth's expression of fidelity composes one of the most beloved portions of Scripture and has secured a place in the Christian tradition, most notably in the marriage ceremony, to express a lifelong commitment.

Ruth said these words to Naomi "on their way to go back to the land of Judah" (v. 7). It is the pivotal moment in the first chapter. It takes place when Ruth and Naomi are between their respective homelands, moving from Ruth's land to Naomi's home. It is when neither one is "at home" that Ruth makes a vow to Naomi that will demand a new understanding of family and home, changing both of their identities forever.

COMMENTARY

"IN THE DAYS THAT THE JUDGES RULED..." (1:1-5)

The story of Ruth begins "in the days that the judges ruled," with a man named Elimelech and his family, which includes his wife, Naomi, and their two sons, Mahlon and Chilion. The family lives in Bethlehem, but a famine forces their migration to Moab. While there, Elimelech dies. The two sons take Moabite wives named Orpah and Ruth. Sometime later, both Mahlon and Chilion die. In the wake of these losses, Naomi receives word that there is now food in Bethlehem and she embarks on her return journey with her two daughters-in-law.

Literary Analysis

The introductory verses of this narrative present the characters, setting, and action of the story. In verse 1, the reader is introduced to a "certain man" who is of Bethlehem in Judah. In this same verse we learn he has a wife and two sons. In addition to their names, this introduction tells us about their geographic location and their family ties. They belong to the tribe of Judah and they are further identified as Ephrathites from Bethlehem. Ephrathah is an established region in Judah. In much the same way we identify ourselves with a first name, a surname, and then a geographic location, this "certain man" comes into focus with each additional bit of information.

Once the main players are identified, the narrative moves quickly and unceremoniously changes the setting. This established family encounters a series of tragedies, beginning with a famine. The crisis of the famine leads to other losses. The family moves because of the famine, and Elimelech dies. The sons marry and then also die. The deaths of the men, who provide for their family, create another type of famine. Now the narrative shifts its attention to Naomi, Elimelech's widow, who will begin the return home.

Exegetical Analysis

The setting and action in the first five verses are wonderful examples of the way Scripture functions on a number of levels. We begin with the setting (time and location) that provides the back-drop for the action. The chapter begins with a temporal reference, "In the days when the judges ruled," approximately thirteenth to twelfth century BCE, before the monarchy. This time marker, along with the concluding genealogy, means the narrative takes place toward the end of Israel's time without a king and anticipates the advent of the monarchy, thus providing a geographical and political setting. In the days of the judges, Israel lived in tension with her surrounding neighbors. A sojourner would be at the mercy of the citizens of the land in which he or she traveled.

It is also the case that "in the days when the judges ruled" there was a pattern of narrative action that is established in the book of Judges. This pattern connected the political life of Israel to its relationship with God. In Judges, the Israelites would forget YHWH and begin worshiping the other gods of the people who surrounded them (2:10b-19). In response to their disobedience, God would "hand them over" to their enemies who oppressed them. The people would cry out to God, who would raise up a judge to deliver them, establishing peace in the land for a period of time, usually a generation, forty years. At the end of that time, the people would forget and pursue other gods, and the cycle would begin again.

In the book of Ruth, there is no mention of a judge, and oppression comes not from another nation but from a famine. Is this a punishment from God because of Israel's disobedience? The famine and the resulting movement into the territory of Moab seem to go against the pattern in Judges where disobedience results in outsider incursion and oppression. Whereas the action in Judges takes place so that Israel will correct her disobedient behavior and worship YHWH only, here the narrative action forces an Israelite family out of its homeland only to return with a Moabite who will become one of the people of Israel.

The action begins in Bethlehem (house of bread). Location takes the foreground as it will be an interpretive lens throughout the narrative. Bethlehem is significant in the history of Israel. Here are a few examples:

1. Bethlehem was taken by the Philistines for a period of time until it was reclaimed by David and made the capital city.

2. In the fifth century BCE, Bethlehem was reoccupied by the returning exiles.
3. Bethlehem is referred to by the prophet Micah as the birthplace of the anointed one or Messiah (Mic 5:2).

The location of the family in a significant city creates some anticipation on the part of the reader. Ephrathah is a name associated with the area around Bethlehem, and it means "fruitful." The additional designation as Ephrathites may serve to strengthen the connection to Bethlehem. Ephrathah is a territory in Judah, and in this context it could refer to a city, district, tribal, or kinship group (Campbell 1975, 55). So the first reference to Elimelech as "a certain man of Bethlehem" suggests this is very likely a well-established Bethlehemite family. And this family, both by virtue of its location and the subsequent action of the narrative, will play a vital role in the story of Israel.

The strong ties to Bethlehem make Elimelech's sojourn to Moab more of a trauma because someone with strong ties to home does not leave easily. The famine is a powerful force, one with the power to uproot and create sojourners out of the well established. Elimelech's sojourn places him in the company of the ancestors Abraham, Isaac, and Jacob, who became sojourners because of famine. In the cases of Abraham and Isaac, there was a very real threat to their families on account of the wives who could have been taken from the husbands (Gen 12; 20; 26). For Abraham, Sarai was twice taken by the ruling monarch because of her beauty, to be saved by some supernatural act of God on her behalf. Jacob and his family settled in Goshen to avoid famine (Gen 46), and his descendents became slaves in that land. In Ruth, the family will move and the family will be in jeopardy, albeit not at the hand of an earthly monarch.

The second location that creates a setting is Moab. Moab is the region of land east of Judah, just on the opposite side of the Dead Sea. The geographic proximity between Israel and Moab speaks to its shared history. Moab is the setting for the book of Deuteronomy—it is where the wandering Israelites camped as they waited to enter the promised land. It is the place where Moses died and was buried.

In spite of its location, the people of Moab are referred to as belonging to "the nations," that is, people who are not Israelites. Although Moab falls into the category of "other," their origins reveal that these people are related to the Israelites. Genesis 19:30-38 chronicles the origins of Moab and Ammon, the sons of Lot, Abraham's nephew. Moab is begotten out the shameful act of incest in Gen 19 between Lot and his daughters. Even though it is close, the land of Moab is not an ideal location to resettle. Either the famine is terrible, or there is something terribly wrong with Elimelech's decision to travel there.

What then are the reasons for Elimelech's journey? The text does not supply one and we are left to come up with our own answers. One solution comes from the genre of the material. An essential element of the comedic plot is movement "from one social center to another" (Frye 1957, 166). So one possibility is that this type of story depends on a shift in location. Another set of possibilities comes from Midrash, the fifth-sixth-century commentary of Ruth called the Ruth Rabbah, which speculates that Elimelech's stature in the community left a void, or perhaps he left to avoid the many requests for help he would have received. This selfish reason for leaving could then be used to justify his untimely death (Nielsen 1997, 18). For postexilic readers, Elimelech's departure from the land would evoke the exile. The Babylonian exile was a selective one. Political leaders, priests, community leaders, and the aristocracy—people like Elimelech—were removed from the land. The extended time in exile meant that many Israelites intermarried and many never returned. All of these possibilities share a basic understanding of leaving the land as undesirable.

The idea that leaving the homeland is a bad idea is supported by its very name. Bethlehem, "house of bread," connotes abundance, not famine. Ephrathah, the region from which Elimelech and his family come, means "fruitful" not barren. Thus for the reader who had no historical knowledge of Bethlehem, its very name signals the audience that leaving the house of bread would only happen under dire circumstances.

Just as the locations in the narrative have names that are replete with meaing, so too do the names of the family introduce a host of narrative possibilities. The name of the patriarch in this family, Elimelech ("my God is king"), can be seen as having meaning not only for the character but also for the entire narrative. God's role as monarch suggests God is in control of the narrative events. It also can be seen as a message that reminds readers that, despite Israel's political status, God is, always and ultimately, king. Naomi ("pleasant") is an appropriate name for a wife and mother of sons in a culture where husbands and sons are the conduits of security and blessing for women. Conversely, with names that mean "sickly" and "destruction," respectively, Mahlon and Chilion will not last long. Orpah's name ("back of neck") will be most appropriate in the narrative action of chapter 1. The names of Ruth ("friend" or "to saturate") and Shaddai ("strength, breast") invite an extended dialogue to determine meaning, and to these we will return. All of the elements that define the characters are subject to the transition of the "sojourn" to the land of Moab where they "remained" (vv. 1-2).

Against the established setting of time, place, and names, the action takes place. Elimelech's move to Moab is the act that precedes tragedy. The text informs us of Elimelech's death with no details on the circumstances regarding his death, stating simply that Naomi was left with her two sons who marry Moabite women (v. 4). Again, there is no detail on the circumstances surrounding these marriages, but the word used for taking a wife is surprising. Usually, the verb used for marrying, literally, "taking a wife" is (*lakah*). In Ruth 1:4, the verb used to describe the marriages of Mahlon and Chilion is not (*lakah*) but (*nasa'*) to "lift up." This verb (*nasa'*) is used to describe the "taking" of wives in Judg 21. In that story, the tribe of Benjamin is judged for its deplorable behavior and a civil war ensues resulting in Benjamin's defeat. None of the tribes of Israel wanted its daughters to marry men from Benjamin. In order to keep Benjamin from dying out, the people decided Benjamin should have wives from Shiloh. The men of Benjamin were instructed to lie in wait, until the young women of Shiloh came out to dance at the yearly festival. The men "carried off" (*nasa'*) virgins to be their wives, thus preventing the line of Benjamin from dying out. Does the use of this verb in Ruth suggest that the marriages between Mahlon, Chilion, and their Moabite wives were less than acceptable? Is it intimating that Orpah and Ruth were "kidnap brides," married to these men against their will, or perhaps that the customs of the Moabites were not regarded in the contracting of these marriages?

In streamlined, determined form, the narrative moves from the death of Elimelech to the marriage of his sons to their death. This is tragedy on a grand scale. Elimelech's death is preceded by leaving the homeland, and his sons' deaths are preceded by marrying foreign women. In Israel's religion, these two acts are major violations of one's core identity, so that the deaths of the men function on literal and symbolic levels.

It is noteworthy that Mahlon and Chilion were married for approximately ten years, because it is plenty of time to have a child. The mention of ten years' time informs us that before the brothers die, there is barrenness. In the ancient world, a woman without sons was in a precarious position. Women inherited property through the men in their lives. A woman without sons had no means of provision if her husband died before she did. From the perspective of the text, it is Naomi (not the Moabite widows) who is bereft.

Theological Analysis

The book of Ruth reflects a cultural construct of identity that is rooted in family, kinship group, tribe, and land. Israel's identity is not simply cultural. It is a theological matter. The Israelites are the family of Abraham, but their covenant with God means that the Israelites are the people of God. Thus the descendants of Abraham use family language and the metaphors of marriage and adoption to describe their relationship with God. This means that whenever something happens to threaten Israel's well-being, there are immediate theological questions that arise. In the book of Ruth, the first five verses are characterized by a famine that results in a sojourn. The movement away from the homeland strips Elimelech and his family of the markers of their identity: land, family ties, and regulations. For the people of God, these events are not simply historical or narrative events. They are theological events that are concerned with what it means to be God's people in dire circumstances.

The famine is the first in the "series of unfortunate events" that strip Naomi of land, husband, continued lineage, and name. Famine is a literal agricultural death and a harbinger of sickness and death for the inhabitants of the land. In the agrarian societies of the ancient Near East, famine had religious connotations. Many cultures (including those surrounding Israel during the time of the judges) believed in deities whose roles were to ensure the production of a crop. The male storm god Baal caused the rain to come in the spring and fertilize the earth, the female deity, allowing the earth to produce grain. A famine would mean that the gods had been unwilling to perform their duties, thus requiring some response from the people who had somehow erred (Robertson 2010, 99-101). This earlier understanding of famine continues to have a symbolic meaning that simply means things are not right.

For Israel, famine was the direct result of YHWH's hand, as it was YHWH who brought rain and harvest. In short, famine was a clear sign that things were not as they should be. In the stories of the ancestors, famine caused Abraham and Isaac to sojourn to other lands where their families faced potential danger because of their wives' beauty. Because this famine is set in the context of the book of Judges, where there is a pattern of sin followed by punishment, a question arises as to whether the famine is punishment for the sin of the people.

In the story of Ruth, the famine forces Elimelech and his family from the ancestral land. In this family- and lineage-based culture, being "cut off" from the land is a type of death. The family is the stronghold against death and the family is rooted to the land. In this sense, the removal from the land is more than a precursor of tragedy, it is a tragedy in itself. Seen in this light, the ensuing deaths of the men can be understood as a direct result of being separated from the land. The land anchors the family and apart from the land there is no safety. An ancient Near Eastern worldview would consider leaving the homeland the equivalent of death, so Elimelech is dead before he dies in the land of Moab. The famine forces Naomi's family out of the land and makes her a widow. Naomi's dilemma is the result of a forced exile and a return many years later. The forced separation from the land and subsequent events left Naomi without markers of her identity structure. With famine comes the loss of life, livelihood, family, and identity. It is easy to see how this catastrophe evokes the experience of the exile for those who return.

A theological reading of these opening verses understands the famine to be both a historical event and something more. Famine evokes a spiritual time of separation. Verse 1 informs the reader that it is the time or season of famine. Thus in this first chapter the reader is reminded of the pain of separation. Inherent in the story of Judah's exile is the longing for restoration. This spiritual separation is effectively conveyed in the language of famine. The devastation of a famine evokes the cognitive dissonance of exile or any experience of separation from God.

Mahlon and Chilion were married for ten years before their deaths, implying barrenness. Like famine, barrenness suggests a lack of God's presence or favor. The fact that the text makes specific mention of ten years as the length of Mahlon's and Chilion's marriages calls to mind the prohibition against the Moabites in Deut 23:3. Does the ten years of childless marriage allude to the exclusion of Moab from the congregation of Israel until the tenth generation? If so, a theological reading may open up the possibility that the ten generations has passed and it is now time to bring Moab back.

"THEN SHE STARTED TO RETURN..." (1:6-18)

In this section, Naomi hears that the famine is over and she leaves for home with her two daughters-in-law. On the way back, she has a change of heart and attempts to sends her daughters-in-law back to their Moabite families. She is only partially successful.

Orpah returns home, but Ruth is undeterred in her decision to stay with Naomi. Ruth expresses her determination to stay in the vow that binds her to Naomi and renews the family ties.

Literary Analysis

Naomi embarks on a second journey when there is food in her homeland, but she will return barren, stripped of the people and things around which her identity was built. The narrative moves between the geographical and symbolic poles of Bethlehem and Moab and the decisive moment in the first chapter takes place between these two locations. For Naomi, Bethlehem is home, the house of bread. It provides sustenance and it represents what is known and safe. Moab is the foil or the counterpart. It is outside the assembly of Israel, unknown and dangerous. In Naomi's own experience, it is the place of death and foreign wives who worship other gods. Thus the journey to Moab is characterized by a stripping away of identity. First, the family leaves its homeland, the place to which its identity is rooted. While its members are sojourners in Moab, Naomi's sons marry Moabite women, which runs counter to their identity as Israelites. Finally, Naomi's husband and sons die and she and these Moabite daughters-in-law lose a primary indicator of identity, the men who inherit on their behalf and provide for them. The deaths of husband and sons are a personal loss as well as a loss of identity for Naomi. In the narrative the deaths result in a shift in emphasis from the men to the women.

This second section of the chapter moves at a much slower pace than the previous five verses and it consists primarily of dialogue. The exchange between the women is a turning point in the chapter and the entire story. There is a literal "turning point," as the widows are at a crossroads and Naomi's daughters-in-law must choose a path. Naomi's words convey a desire to be alone. Orpah concedes to Naomi's wishes but Ruth refuses to leave.

The tragedy of the husbands' deaths makes Naomi the focal point of the loss. She is isolated by circumstances, but as her words suggest Naomi also sees herself utterly desolate. This isolation, in literary terms, is a characteristic of tragedy. In verses 8-13, Naomi refers to herself eleven times. She understands herself to be utterly alone and without hope. Sending her daughters-in-law away is the right response to her desolation and lack of hope. However, Ruth's decision not to leave forces a change in Naomi's reality, if not her perception. The literal turning point results in a literary turning point. Ruth returns with Naomi because she will not be dissuaded. Naomi's future will not be faced alone, but she returns to Bethlehem much changed by recent events. As a result, the narrative follows the story of Naomi and Ruth, not that of Naomi in isolation. What was a potential tragedy now follows the path of comedy.

Exegetical Analysis

Now the narrative focuses on Naomi, who is on her way back home. She is widowed and bereft of her sons, but she has heard that there is food in the land of Judah, her home. Verse 6 contains the phrase "the country of Moab" twice. She begins to return from Moab because she heard (in Moab) that the LORD had "given [his people] food," literally, bread. What is of note is that Naomi heard of the work of the lord in a strange land. Like the material that precedes it, there is narrative action, but it is slower, with a bit more detail. For example, verses 6 and 7 indicate the beginning of an action. In verse 6, she "started to return." In verse 7, she "set out from the place where she had been living." After ten years of living in Moab, Naomi is finally able to return home.

With Naomi's return comes the question, what happens in the wake of tragedy when people survive but the people, places, and customs that mark their identity are gone? This dilemma informs Naomi's behavior when she is on her way out of Moab and on her way to Bethlehem. She returns home stripped of everything that made her Naomi. She is literally and figuratively at a crossroads. Moreover, she is faced with an ethical dilemma. Mahlon's and Chilion's intermarriage is in direct violation of Israelite law. What is Naomi's correct response: to send her daughters-in-law away or bring them home? What would have happened if

Mahlon and Chilion had lived? Would they have put away their foreign, childless wives before returning to Bethlehem? Naomi's behavior confirms that she has been shaped by a particular construct of identity. When she is stripped of the trappings of the construct, she still clings to the ideals of the construct.

With two references to the return in verses 6 and 7, the narrative movement begins with three people on the journey. They "set out" for Bethlehem in verse 7, but verse 8 reads like an interruption or a change of heart: "But Naomi said to her two daughters-in-law, 'Go back each of you to your mother's house.'"

These are the first words spoken by a character in the narrative. The verse begins with the conjunction *waw* that is translated as "but," indicating the contrast between the departure for home and Naomi's words, which reflect a delay in the action, and a change in plans. The conjunction signals more than a simple shift in the narrative; this particular time it introduces *the moment* when a decisive movement takes place. This moment/movement is the piece of the chapter around which the rest of the elements orbit. Here the dialogue that is central to the narrative takes place.

Dialogue between women is an uncommon occurrence in Scripture (Tull 2003, 53). Most often, the conversations recorded in Scripture between women concern men. The book of Ruth stands out not only because of the number of conversations between women (six of the ten conversations in the book are between women and five of those six are between Naomi and Ruth) but also because of their length and the breadth of the subject matter. Ruth and Naomi's conversations reflect concern about each other. Even if by default, this time the focus is not on the men.

Naomi instructs her daughters-in-law, "Go back" (v. 8). The word used here, *sub*, appears nine times in this section (1:6-18), and means "turn back," "return," "go," or "come back," even "turn away" or "put" or "bring back." Clearly Naomi is returning home after sojourning in a strange land, but her return is complicated by the fact that instead of returning with the men in her life, around whom her identity was formed, she embarks on her journey home as a widow, accompanied by two more widows, and these widows are Moabites. From Naomi's perspective, she is utterly alone, and the presence of her daughters-in-law does not alter the fact that she is utterly "bereft."

Both Naomi and her daughters-in-law use the term "return" (*sub*) to describe the action of return. When Naomi uses it, she does so in reference to her daughters-in-law going back home to Moab. When Ruth and Orpah first use it, they use it to state that they will "return back with her." This is an odd usage of the term for the Moabites because they cannot return to a place they have never been. Perhaps the emphasis is on "with," meaning that they will accompany Naomi on her return to her land. Another possibility is that when they use the word *sub*, they invoke the sense of the word that would suggest turning their backs on their homeland and going in another direction. Yet another possibility is that they will return as representatives for their husbands. This recurring use of the verb *sub* highlights the fact that Naomi is returning home while Orpah and Ruth are not.

Particularly noteworthy is the pattern established by the occurrences of *sub*. In verse 6, Naomi *returns,* she and her daughters-in-law. In verse 7, she returned. In verse 8, Naomi commands the two young women to *return*. In verse 10, the daughters-in-law reply that they will *return* (plural) with her. In verse 11, Naomi repeats the command that her daughters-in-law *return* (plural), and again in verse 12. In verse 15, *return* appears in the singular—this time Naomi is commenting on the fact that Orpah has *turned back,* and in verse 16, the word appears again to refer to one person, Ruth.

The place of this exchange is significant. Naomi instructs Orpah and Ruth to turn back after the journey has begun. It could be argued that she instructs them to turn back at a "crossroads" of sorts. Naomi, Orpah, and Ruth are family because of marriage, and in this case intermarriage is forbidden. The marriages that were tolerated in the land of Moab will not go unnoticed in Bethlehem. In that sense, Naomi has reached the geographical limits of having Moabite daughters-in-law. Although Ruth and Orpah were not strangers in the land of

Moab, they would most certainly be in Bethlehem. Naomi, now a widow without sons, may not want the additional burden of foreign daughters that no respectable Israelite would marry. Geography affects identity.

At the crossroads, this no-man's-land, anything can happen. Without the moorings of location, the intention of Naomi's words is full of possibility. Does Naomi instruct her daughters-in-law to return because of concern for them or out of concern for herself? The argument Naomi uses to convince the young women to go back to their mother's homes speaks to her inability to provide husbands for them. In one sense, her words speak to their well-being. The text maintains a perspective that centers on Naomi's loss: she is bereft of husband, sons, and the prospect of another husband. As difficult as the situation for Ruth and Orpah might be, "it has been far more bitter" for Naomi because, "the hand of the LORD has turned against me" (v. 13).

Orpah, like Ruth, weeps at the thought of being separated from her mother-in-law, but she does eventually return to her mother's home. Scholars have traditionally seen Orpah as a foil to Ruth. Orpah leaves her mother-in-law and Ruth stays, which makes Orpah appear to love Naomi less or at least be less faithful than Ruth. Since we cannot know Orpah's reasons for leaving, we must be careful in our interpretation. Ruth's decision to stay with Naomi is peculiar to many traditions, but to others, it is standard behavior. A community of Kenyan women who reads Ruth understood Ruth's actions to be nothing but faithful and obedient. Many Kenyan cultures would understand that "marriage is for-ever—to a family, not to an individual" (Dube 2001, 179). Through the lens of this community, Ruth's decision would make sense because the husband's death would not release the widow from the dead man's family. Read this way, it is possible that Naomi's words are perfunctory—that she offers her daughters-in-law the opportunity to go home, but does not expect them to accept the offer. In this interpretive scenario, Orpah's decision is one of a faithful daughter to her own mother, people, and gods. Another possibility is that Naomi is doing something remarkable by sending the women home. It also explains the force of the repetition in her commands to return. She is going against the cultural grain by sending them back. She is offering them a gift, which Orpah accepts.

If the greatest tragedy of a family- and lineage-based culture is being cut off from the family, we can understand Ruth's resistance to Naomi's command as a survival tactic. In other words, Ruth's decision to cling to Naomi makes sense if Ruth understands Naomi to be her primary family now. The divergent paths of Orpah and Ruth may be nothing more than a reflection of how each woman defines herself—which family she chooses for her primary affiliation. For Ruth, the bond is not severed, even under the most extreme circumstances, and for Orpah, the extenuating circumstances of all the men's deaths allows for her to return home. If that is the case, it is possible to read Naomi's command to return as an opportunity for her daughters-in-law to choose an identity. This is a gift that would be rare in this culture. Whether the rules dictate that the widow stays or that she returns home, these cultures would have a precedent. Naomi's command offers self-determination. Orpah and Ruth get to choose the house, lineage, and name to which they belong. This would also explain why the encounter takes place in the liminal space on the road between one land and another. In this in-between space, Orpah and Ruth have an opportunity to choose the family name.

As such, both daughters are faithful, only to different homes. This also reminds the reader that for all the indicators that a community uses to construct identity, there is always some amount of choice about which constructs we choose to take on. Orpah chooses to be faithful to her mother's house and Ruth to that of her mother-in-law.

The meaning of Orpah's name, "back of neck," may be a clue to help us interpret Orpah's choice. The name "back of neck" evokes the image of two individuals in dialogue. When we face each other, we see the world behind the other's head that that person is unable to see. For this reason, dialogue is essential to a broader understanding. The persons with whom we engage in dialogue have a view beyond ours and we have a view beyond theirs. Whether her reasons are good or not, when Orpah turns away, she is no longer in dialogue. Ruth and Naomi go in a different direction and the three women no longer have a shared range of perspective. Orpah is cut off in the narrative and we cannot know her story. Perhaps the tragedy of Orpah's departure, if there is one, is simply that.

That we cannot know Orpah's story does not prevent listeners from creating one. One very interesting tradition surrounding Orpah is that she traveled four miles with Naomi before deciding to turn back to Moab where she "abandoned herself to an immoral life." However, she was rewarded for traveling four miles with Naomi with four sons who were giants, one of whom was Goliath (Ginzberg 1956, 518). What this tradition does is extend its understanding of Orpah as a foil to Ruth. Since Ruth will eventually become the ancestress of David, Orpah, who turned away, will be the ancestress of the giant that David slew in battle.

Naomi again tries to convince Ruth to return by pointing out that Orpah has returned (v. 15). In response to this argument, Ruth offers a vow:

> Do not press me to leave you
> or to turn back from following you!
> Where you go, I will go;
> where you lodge, I will lodge;
> your people shall be my people,
> and your God my God.
> Where you die, I will die—
> there will I be buried.
> May the LORD do thus and so to me,
> and more as well,
> if even death parts me from you! (vv. 16-17)

Ruth's response begins with a negative command and moves to a series of positive proclamations. Structurally, Ruth's words consist of a series of doublets (paired lines) that ends in a vow. Ruth will identify with Naomi, with her location, people, and God in life and death. The first doublet carries more force than ordinary prose. It carries the strength of a command. The language of the next two doublets in verse 16 starts with Naomi and then with Ruth, emphasizing the action of following. Ruth will return with Naomi back to Jerusalem. The structure of Ruth's vow makes it clear that Ruth intends to follow "after" Naomi:

> You (Naomi) go/I go;
> you (Naomi) lodge/I lodge;
> your (Naomi's) people/my people:
> your (Naomi's) God/my god;
> you (Naomi) die/I die.

From a literary perspective, Naomi is the point of reference for Ruth's action. Ruth's life is bound to Naomi. Ruth takes on Naomi's God because Ruth is committed to Naomi. The vow that concludes this segment demonstrates that Ruth is not simply expressing a desire; by invoking the name of Naomi's God, she is taking a stand, and in response, Naomi "said no more" (v. 18). Ruth's invoking of YHWH's name is bold. After all, YHWH's name is sacred for Israelites, invoked only when taking the most solemn of vows. Under what circumstances would someone other than an Israelite use the name of the most high God?

The exegetical analysis reveals that the center òf the chapter, the exchange between Naomi and Ruth, is not only the center of chapter 1 but also of the entire book. Ruth's decision to stay is the action upon which the rest of the narrative action hangs. In the center of this first chapter we observe a convergence of location, narrative action, characters, and time. It is what Oprah (not Orpah) calls the "aha!" moment.

In Ruth, these "aha!" moments exist in the public sphere and in the unknown world. The first decisive moment takes place in the liminal space between Moab and Judah where there are no men, momentarily outside the reach of a patriarchal society. Here the women are severed from their geographic identity and their familial ties. In the absence of these all-important trappings of identity, Ruth makes a vow, a covenant, with Naomi. The vow that is made in secret is not only determinative for the action in that chapter but also for the entire narrative. Ruth's words are performative speech (Austin 1962, 5). They call into being something that is not, in the same way that the words "I take thee..." in a marriage ceremony speak a reality into being.

Each chapter has a decisive moment, one that determines the direction of the narrative, but Ruth's vow in chapter 1 is arguably the turning point for the chapter and the entire narrative. A vow is made in an unknown place between two widows, each of whom would be unrecognizable in the other's context. Ruth's commitment to Naomi restores a family that had been decimated by death. The marriage that tied Ruth to Naomi has been destroyed by death. Ruth's vow affirms an understanding of family that is informed by faithfulness (*hesed*), which by definition knows no bounds.

Ruth's words form a new reality, a new family, and a new identity. It is covenant. Covenant is a contract enacted between two entities that expresses the existence and the nature of their commitment to each other. The covenants of the Sinai legislation resemble the "suzerain" treaties in which the "suzerain" or lord enacts a treaty with a defeated enemy who is now vassal or slave. In such a treaty, the lord states who he is and his many accomplishments that affirm his position as such. This is followed by the conditions of the treaty that are then followed by a vow that invokes blessings if the covenant is followed and curses if it is not. In his discussion of the Sinai covenant, Jon Levenson compares God's covenant with Israel to a *ketubbah,* a wedding contract (Levenson, 1985, 75). The juxtaposition of a suzerain/vassal treaty and a *ketubbah* is instructive because the suzerain/vassal treaty is clearly between unequals. Ruth defers to Naomi in this dialogue. She places Naomi first: "You go...I go, and so forth." Although Ruth defers to Naomi, she is not a conquered vassal. She enters into this commitment with Naomi of her own free will and this element evokes the *ketubbah* because under the best of circumstances, the *ketubbah* is a contract that has the expectation of love.

Ruth's words are powerful because of what they do. Vows do not simply describe a new reality, they invoke it. The words of a vow have the power to change things. Around Ruth's words there are two realities: one before the vow and another after. In response to Naomi's offer of release, Ruth gets married all over again. Her commitment is sealed by the reference to her place of burial, identifying herself with Naomi's people.

Ruth's incorporation into this Israelite family entails an adoption of religious values and practices. As such, the values of family ties to land, the continuation of the line, and the memory of the dead are foundational in this story. Biblical Israel upheld the widespread cultural belief that the preservation of family was a response to and a defense against death. Kinship and community ties extend beyond the grave and familial property. Burial places bore witness to the ongoing ties of family (Cook 2009, 112). This cultural value was wed to the religious value of "faithfulness" (*hesed*), which connoted God's faithfulness to Israel and the expectation of Israel's faithfulness to God through covenant (Cook 2009, 117). Because the concept of *hesed* is integral to the story of Ruth, a detailed definition of this term is in order.

Hesed is an act that preserves or promotes life. It is often translated as faithfulness, loving-kindness, steadfast love, grace, or goodness. The range of usage demonstrates that *hesed* is relational; it is used to describe a type of interaction between two entities, most often, but not limited relatives. Sometimes it refers to a relationship between a sovereign and subjects, or two unrelated parties. *Hesed* is active; it is more than an attitude. It is something that is demonstrated. It is related to the concept of "doing good" or "commandment." The usage of *hesed* in Scripture also reveals an expectation of mutuality in the "doing" of *hesed*. One act of this faithfulness encourages and inspires more of the same. Thus this *hesed* is active, social, and enduring.

Of the 124 times that *hesed* has a possessive suffix, 113 of these refer to YHWH. YHWH "gives" *hesed,* "sends" *hesed,* "remembers" *hesed,* "continues" *hesed,* and "shows" *hesed.* God can also take away *hesed.* God's acts of *hesed* toward Israel characterize God's nature because God's *hesed* is everlasting. It is the thing about God that Israel depends upon. In the psalms of lament the psalmist pleads with God to remember his faithfulness/*hesed,* and in songs of praise God's everlasting *hesed* is celebrated throughout history (Ps 136:1-26).

The usage of *hesed* makes a clear case that it is one of God's most memorable characteristics. It is what enables humans to have a relationship with God, and it is what allows for the renewal of relationships when things go wrong. God's faithfulness to Israel has no limits or boundaries. In fact, God's faithfulness extends beyond Israel to the whole earth (Ps 36:5). Over and over again, Scripture attests to the limitless nature of God's *hesed*. By incorporating the notion of *hesed* with kinship and family practices, Israel makes the practice of faithfulness within a family a divine attribute (Cook 2009, 115). What results is a commitment that is not limited by death. If death does not mark the limits of *hesed*, neither do existing constructs of identity. In light of the limitless nature of God's *hesed* we should expect to find it in new, unexpected places.

Although they are two distinct concepts, faithfulness (*hesed*) and covenant are interrelated. *Hesed* is an act that is not limited to covenant or members of a covenant community. However, a covenant is defined by *hesed*. Thus Ruth and Orpah demonstrate this faithfulness to their husbands outside of the covenant community. When Ruth makes a vow to Naomi, she ratifies a relationship that already existed because of faithfulness.

There are noteworthy features to Ruth's oath in verse 17: "May the LORD do thus and so to me, and more as well, if even death parts me from you!" Ruth never names a penalty in the oath. The consequences of breaking the oath are so terrible they are unspeakable. Other oaths in the Bible are uttered by a king or a leader and they have weighty consequences (1 Sam 14:44; 2 Sam 3:9; and 1 Kgs 2:23) (Davis and Parker 2003, 31). In making this oath, Ruth makes her decision weighty and serious—the genre of the oath makes it so.

It is no small thing that Ruth invokes the name of Naomi's god. Invoking the divine name in a vow is the argument to which Naomi has no response. In taking on a vow with the divine name, Ruth has passed the point of no return. She is willing to put her life on the line to stay with Naomi. Does she risk her life by taking on this vow as a Moabite in the first place?

Another foreign woman who uses the divine name is Rahab in

Josh 2:9 when she speaks to the spies she has hidden: "I know that the LORD has given you the land, and that dread of you has fallen on us, and that all the inhabitants of the land melt in fear before you." In both of these instances, the speakers evoke the divine name in a provocative way. In Joshua, Rahab, a foreigner, confirms the promises of God to deliver Jericho to the Israelites, and in Ruth, this Moabite invokes God's name in a vow as a demonstration of *hesed,* faithfulness, which is a characteristic of God.

Ruth invokes YHWH's name to make a vow that binds her to Naomi in death a well as in life. This commitment reflects the cultural value of family and its inexorable connection to land. It is through the maintenance of family that death is kept at bay. This family maintenance includes the preservation of the family tomb. Ruth's reference to a bond to Naomi in death means that she will work with Naomi to preserve the family name of the dead, and she will take on the ultimate mark of a family member: burial in the family plot (Cook 2009, 117). This commitment to remembering the dead and ensuring the continuation of the line is one definition of *hesed.* Ruth's vow then entails maintaining the family, those living and dead.

The vow formula "so may God do..." appears twelve times in Scripture. Of these twelve occurrences YHWH's name is invoked twice. One is here in Ruth's vow to Naomi and the other is in Jonathan's vow to David (1 Sam 20:13) (Campbell 1975, 74). Like the vow Ruth made to Naomi, Jonathan's vow to David maintains family ties when they are threatened. In the example of David and Jonathan there are the elements of marriage, family, identity, and rights. Saul was the king chosen by God and later rejected. God subsequently chose David who came under Saul's employ as a musician and served in the army of Israel. As David became of increased value to the kingdom, Saul gave his daughter Michal to David in marriage. This is an example of a practical if not shrewd reason for marriage. The union of David and Michal keeps David close by Saul, and a part of his house. David would be far more reluctant to lead an uprising against his father-in-law. Moreover, if Michal bears David a son, the houses would have an heir in common. Unfortunately, the practical benefits of their marriage were never realized (2 Sam 6:20-23).

First Samuel 18:1 tells us the Jonathan loved David "as his own soul." Out of this devotion, Jonathan made a covenant with David and his descendants. It is this vow that leads David to search for Jonathan's descendants with the intention of "show[ing] kindness" (2 Sam 9:1). Although it stands to reason that David's gathering of Jonathan's descendants may also have had a political motivation, the point I want to make here is that in the absence of an heir from a political/practical marriage, the vow between David and Jonathan, which came out of love, acts as a familial bond between David and Jonathan's sons.

It should be noted that in the examples of Ruth and Naomi and David and Jonathan, the vow is made between individuals after a traditional union failed to produce offspring. David's marriage to Michal, Saul's daughter, did not result in an heir. Had a child been born to David and Michal, the tension between the house of Saul and that of David would have been resolved. As the narrative unfolds, it can be argued that God had no intention of continuing with the line of Saul and wanted to establish a new house. Thus in the David story, the covenant between Jonathan and David facilitates the transfer of God's favor from one family to another. In the case of the covenant between Ruth and Naomi, the vow facilitates the expansion of God's favor from a particular people to include an "outsider."

Theological Analysis

The first two sections of chapter 1 chronicle two journeys—the first is away from home, which evokes sojourning and exile, and the second is toward home, which evokes the entry into the land and the return. The second journey evokes both exodus and the return from exile. On the way home, Naomi offers her Moabite daughters-in-law a choice in a context where almost all of their choices were made for them. The choice, inherent in the command to go home, evokes Joshua's challenge to the tribes of Israel toward the end of his tenure as their leader; "choose this day whom you will serve" (Josh 24:15). As is the case at key moments in the Deuteronomistic History, there is the presence of a speech that recounts God's faithfulness and asks the people to affirm their commitment (i.e., covenant) with YHWH. The Ruth story adds a twist to that format. In Ruth's story the people are not triumphant. Nevertheless they are offered an opportunity to choose, and here, return home.

The motif of pausing to create or affirm a covenant serves a theological purpose. A covenant makes God's relationship with Israel official. It is the means by which Israel becomes God's family, be it through marriage or adoption. The repetition of the covenant motif reminds us that God's covenant is ongoing. Deuteronomy asserts that each generation must choose to make the covenant with God for itself. Each time a covenant is made in the narrative, the audience remembers that God has been faithful and God will be faithful. Going forward in this unknown territory, the narrative evokes the familiar motif of covenant to remind the character and the audience that God's faithfulness remains in a changing world.

God's faithfulness is evoked both in the covenant and in the mention of the divine name, YHWH. This is the God who called Israel into being as a people and a nation—this God's very name, "I am becoming what I am becoming," is filled with possibility.

This particular covenant is theologically curious because although the words are "right," the setting and characters are wrong. On what basis does a Moabite woman make a covenant with an Israelite woman? If we compare Ruth's vow with a suzerain vassal treaty, a complex analogy becomes evident. On one hand, Ruth is the vassal because she submits to Naomi. On the other hand, she is the suzerain because she enacts the treaty and because she is free to choose. She can return home to Moab or continue with Naomi to Bethlehem. Moreover, based on their current reality, Ruth stands to lose by making a commitment to Naomi in the same way that God makes God's self vulnerable by entering into covenant with Israel. When God makes a covenant with Israel, God is "marrying down."

Ruth's words reach across the constructs of her world and Naomi's. Her vow envisions a familial relationship that was unheard of before. The only thing that holds Naomi and Ruth together is this dialogue. Ruth's pledge to Naomi is the narrative and theological "glue" of the story.

For a people attempting to construct a religious identity, Ruth reminds her audiences that YHWH's people are not only chosen, they must choose YHWH. One part of that choice is reflected in the making of the covenant that requires fidelity.

"CALL ME NO LONGER NAOMI..." (1:19-22)

Naomi arrives in Bethlehem with her Moabite daughter-in-law at the beginning of the barley harvest and their arrival causes a stir. "Is this Naomi?" the women of the town ask, and Naomi responds out of her pain, telling them not to call her Naomi, meaning "full/pleasant" but Mara, meaning "bitter, because the Almighty has dealt bitterly with me" (1:20).

Literary Analysis

The first chapter begins in Bethlehem with a famine and ends in Bethlehem at the beginning of the harvest and here the story will stay for the remainder of the book. In this final section there is tension between the promise of harvest and the emptiness that Naomi embodies. If we read the story metaphorically, then Naomi is Israel returning from exile, bereft of all that she had, with this new baggage of a foreign woman/wife. If identity is tied to location then we know the identity of Ruth and Naomi will be tied to Bethlehem.

In this final section, the narrative action resumes as "the two of them" (Naomi and Ruth) "went on until they came to Bethlehem" (v. 19). The mention of the number two reminds the reader of all those who have not returned by choice (Orpah) or with no choice (Elimelech, Mahlon, and Chilion). Moreover, the names mentioned in this final section take the reader back to the names of the family listed at the beginning and reflect the changes that have transpired. Naomi changes her name to "Mara," meaning bitter. Naomi wants to identify with her loss and does not acknowledge the young woman accompanying her. When she is acknowledged by the narrative, Ruth, her daughter-in-law, has something added to her name. She is now Ruth "the Moabite." This qualifier was unnecessary when she was in Moab, but now in Bethlehem she is officially an outlier. Another name that warrants our attention is the one invoked for God in this final section, "Shaddai," and to this we shall return in the following sections.

Exegetical Analysis

These two are an odd couple, an Israelite widow and a Moabite widow, connected by marriage to dead men and Ruth's vow. The strangeness of this pair and the circumstances that bind them (famine, marriage, death) are apparently reflected in their appearance as well: "When they came to Bethlehem, the whole town was stirred because of them; and the women said, 'Is this Naomi?' " What is it about Naomi that causes "the whole town" to be "stirred"? Has her appearance been altered by her suffering? Is it the passage of time that contributes to their uncertainty? Is it who accompanies or who no longer accompanies her? After all, Naomi left with a husband and two sons and returned with a strange woman. The question itself, "Is this Naomi?" is a phrase that indicates some level of memory and recognition (after all, they are guessing that it is Naomi). It suggests that there are elements of her appearance that are consistent with their memory of Naomi and elements that are inconsistent with their memory of her. In other words, the question acknowledges substantive changes. Whatever the basis for the question, Naomi answers with clear direction:

> "Call me no longer Naomi [Pleasant],
> call me Mara [Bitter],
> for the Almighty [Shaddai] has dealt
> bitterly with me."

Here, as in 1:2, the significance of the names allows us to read the narrative on a historical and metaphorical level. Naomi insists on a change in name that reflects her change in identity from pleasant to bitter, and from full to barren. Usually, a change in name reflects growth, expansion, and development. Unlike the majority of passages where names have been changed, Naomi initiates this change in form of address. Moreover, she uses another name for God, heretofore not used in this narrative.

Based on this easy association between Naomi's names and her status, the reader's attention is drawn to the name Shaddai ("for Shaddai has dealt harshly with me"), which, unlike the names Naomi and Mara, does not have a simple meaning or association. Like the other "El" names, Shaddai is a title that speaks to some aspect of God. Shaddai is most readily translated to connote strength that leads to the translation of "God Almighty." A very strong argument based on cognate languages has been made that "Shaddai" could connote breasts. As such, the title for YHWH would be the "breasted one." In a text that focuses on women and themes of famine and infertility, this is certainly an intriguing option. In the ancient Near Eastern context, the breast symbolizes the ability to nurture and provide sustenance that is the power to sustain life. In the surrounding cultures, breasts would evoke goddesses who were often formidable warriors. In short, the connotation of "Shaddai" as "breasted one" does not limit possible interpretations but expands them.

In these final verses of chapter 1, Ruth, Naomi's daughter-in-law, also takes on a title: "So Naomi returned together with Ruth the Moabite, her daughter-in-law, who came back with her from the country of Moab. They came to Bethlehem at the beginning of the barley harvest" (v. 22). Ruth has become "the Moabite." In Naomi's land, she has become "other." The shift in her location has affected her identity and this shift in identity has come with a shift in the season. In these final verses, Naomi has returned to the place of her origins as has the narrative. The famine has been replaced with the time of harvest and her family has been replaced with "the Moabite." The title "the Moabite" is followed by another title, "her daughter-in-law."

One speaks to her status as an outsider and the other identifies her as family. The shift in location raises the question of which title will hold sway in the narrative action. The literary contrast is intriguing. There is loss alongside the hope that comes with harvest. Within the character of Ruth there is foreigner and family, loss and hope.

Naomi's return to Bethlehem results in a question of identity. The people's question, "Is this Naomi?" evokes both a sense of knowing and not knowing. The question includes her name, suggesting they recognize her enough to call her name. The first part of the question, "is this" suggests there is enough about her that has changed so that the question needs to be asked. It is an attempt at recognition and identification.

The encounter has two components. The first is coming together, the meeting, and the second is the moment of identifying each other. When we encounter another person, there is an instant, a very brief passing of time, when we move from simply seeing another person to perceiving him or her as someone who is known or unknown. In scientific terms this is described as memory/recognition. When we see another person, our brains quickly go through the catalog of stored images from memory to find a match. The images in our brains not only record images of people but also their contexts. This may explain why the townswomen ask, "Is this Naomi?" The question highlights the fluidity of identity. It may have been that parts of what they encountered matched their memory of her and parts did not.

In literary terms this discernment/determination of one as known or unknown is the moment of recognition/nonrecognition. There are certain motifs, such as meeting/parting, loss/acquisition, search/discovery, recognition/nonrecognition that serve as repositories of meaning within a text (Bakhtin 1981, 97). Of these motifs, the motif of meeting provides us with the opportunity to see and discern, and recognize another as foreigner or family.

When we meet or encounter another, in a matter of seconds we determine how we know the other person and who this person is. The response of the people to Naomi upon her return highlights the fluidity of identity. Here they meet Naomi but the question acknowledges change has taken place. Why is Naomi hard to recognize?

This notion of identity being shaped by outside factors is inherent in the vocabulary of "other" or "foreigner" in Hebrew. The word for foreigner, "*nakri,*" is related to the verbal root, *nakar,* to recognize. "Other" or "outsider" is someone who is recognized as such. This raises the question, what characteristics determine "other," and what constructs are in place in any given culture to designate the other?

The return to the land in this final section reminds the reader that the land has a role to play in the story. Like the characters, the land has experienced a famine at the beginning of the chapter and moves to a time of harvest at the end. The land is central to Israel's identity and the repetition of Naomi's command to return, *sub,* evokes the longing of those exiled in subsequent generations to come home. On a literary level, the famine symbolized the land's longing to be full; for all of her inhabitants to return. The famine is the call of Israel because she is incomplete, and she longs for the return of all her children. The children who are to return include more than the members of the Jewish diaspora. The sojourn of Elimelech serves as a means of bringing the daughter of Moab, or daughter Moab, back to the land.

The phrase that concludes the first chapter, "at the beginning of the barley harvest," is like the opening phrase, a temporal one. The harvest is counter to the famine, signaling a change is imminent. Harvest connotes abundance and plentitude, an antidote to Naomi's identity based in lack and loss. She returns at a time of harvest and the person who accompanies her will literally bear the fruit of the harvest. An allegorical reading of the names has "pleasant" Naomi and "saturate" Ruth returning to the "fruitful" region (Ephrathah) of the "house of Bread" (Bethlehem).

Theological Analysis

In the wake of Hurricane Katrina, Americans observed the numerous dilemmas faced by its victims. The survivors of the storm left home for their own safety only to return weeks later to a "home" that had changed. As a result, many discovered they themselves had changed. For those who suffered losses, there were a myriad of questions to be answered, including, do I return? Should I stay with no guarantee of a job? Do I rebuild? If so, should I rebuild in the same area? These questions reflect some larger ones, including, what is central to one's sense of self or identity? For some residents of the affected areas in Mississippi and Louisiana, the neighborhood had value, while for others it was the city itself, or their property. Others chose family or employment over location, which allowed them to move away. These choices are not easily made, rather they reflect the resources and the core values of the people who made them.

For Israel, the land has always been central to identity, although many significant moments in its story occurred outside of the land. There is an inherent tension in Israel's identity between the people who wandered and experienced God's presence and the people who understand the land is proof of God's presence.

The confusion around Naomi's identity upon her return speaks to Israel's identity crisis upon her return to the land after exile. She has returned to the land that is central to her identity but she is no longer the same; she has lost so much and what she has is foreign. When Naomi instructs the women to call her "Mara" she gives voice to Israel after exile. Her primary identity is that of loss and emptiness at the hand of "Shaddai." Before she can rebuild, Naomi and the nation she represents must mourn what has been lost.

Interestingly, the answer to the question of identity is in the name for God that Naomi invokes. Shaddai speaks to God's omnipotence and God's ability to nurture and sustain. Even in the midst of her confusion around her identity, the mention of Shaddai contains hope. Shaddai is the key to Naomi's identity. Shaddai overshadows Naomi's bitterness. The other irony is that the faithfulness of Shaddai is represented by the presence of Ruth. Although the focus in this final section is on Naomi, and Ruth is practically invisible, it is through the young Moabitess that God will demonstrate God's faithfulness for God's beloved people.

CHAPTER 2
TERMS OF ENDEARMENT

Ruth becomes "the Moabite" when she leaves Moab for Judah, but her decision to cling to Naomi brings her into the presence of a wealthy kinsman named Boaz. In chapter 1, we observed that identity is influenced by one's location. In this second chapter, we observe that kinship is more than blood. Ruth's ties to Naomi in spite of her "otherness" are reflected in her description as both Moabite and daughter-in-law. Her faithfulness, not her ancestry, becomes a determining factor in the shaping of her identity.

"NOW NAOMI HAD A KINSMAN . . ." (2:1-3)

Ruth goes out to gather behind the harvesters (a practice called gleaning) so that she and Naomi can eat. As luck would have it, she finds herself gleaning in the field of one of Naomi's relatives named Boaz.

Literary Analysis

Three parts compose this second chapter of the Ruth narrative. First there is Ruth and Naomi's survival plan in verses 1-3, followed by a central section of dialogue (vv. 4-16), and then the results of the plan at the end of the chapter (vv. 17-23).

Like the first section of chapter 1, the first section of chapter 2 provides us with a new setting and an introduction of a new character, Boaz, who will support the dialogue and action in the middle of the chapter. In verse 1 the narrator addresses the audience, providing the reader with insider information—facts that are yet unknown to Ruth: "Now Naomi had a kinsman on her husband's side, a prominent rich man, of the family of Elimelech, whose name was Boaz."

The narrator supplies this information at the beginning of the chapter, thereby creating a sense of anticipation on the part of the reader. If we read through a comedic lens, we will expect coincidental meetings and mistaken identity as a part of the story. What role will Boaz play in the development of the narrative? Does he know Naomi has returned, and is he in a position to help? If so, will he?

Exegetical Analysis

Boaz's introduction is similar to that of Elimelech in chapter 1, in that he is revealed in stages, with his name given last.

Ruth 1:1-2	Ruth 2:1
A certain man	a kinsman on husband's side
from Bethlehem in Judah	a prominent rich man
a wife and two sons	belonging to the family of Elimelech
Elimelech	Boaz

In much the same way that Elimelech comes into focus with each additional identifying marker, so does Boaz. There are two references to Boaz's family ties. The first reference is "a kinsman on her husband's side" and the second is "of the family of Elimelech." Not only is he a kinsman (potential help) but he is also prominent and rich (clearly has the power to help), belongs to the family of Elimelech (potential husband?), and, finally, has the name Boaz, which in Hebrew means "in strength." The name also means architect and donor. When Solomon built the Temple he placed two pillars on either side of the vestibule and the name of the pillar on the north side of the Temple vestibule is Boaz. Knowing Boaz's identity provides the reader with a clue to the ensuing action. The audience grasps the significance of Ruth's location before she does. What could be deemed coincidence is providential to the informed reader. He is one who could play a role in the building up of Elimelech's house.

The information in verse 1 is followed by the narrative in verses 2 and 3. When Ruth seeks Naomi's permission to "glean ... behind someone in whose sight I may find favor," in verse 2, the reader has an idea who that "someone" may be.

Naomi's simple response signals some changes that have taken place between chapter 1 and chapter 2. "Go, my daughter" reminds us of Naomi's command to Ruth and Orpah in chapter 1, "Turn back, my daughters" (1:11, 12). In this new location, Naomi sends Ruth out but not to send her away. Ruth's vow has changed everything. As Naomi's kin she will go out to provide for their family. In chapter 1, Naomi was concerned with finding security for her daughters-in-law. In chapter 2, Ruth, her daughter-in-law, goes out to seek provisions for them.

Ruth's plan to go out and glean also evokes the journey motif that we have already seen in this narrative. In chapter 1, the famine forces a family from its homeland to find food elsewhere. The migration for food and water is fraught with danger, as the experience of Sudanese and Congolese women in our current time demonstrates. In this chapter, Ruth leaves the home in Bethlehem to find a field where she may glean and procure food for the family. Although on a smaller scale, the narrative movement in chapter 2, like that in chapter 1, is motivated by the need for food. The journeys of Naomi in chapter 1, and that of Ruth in chapter 2, result in encounters that transform their identities.

Ruth gleans in verse 3 and "as luck would have it" (*TANAKH*), she comes to Boaz's field. The phrase suggests this is an unplanned occurrence. It connotes an accident, chance, or fortune. Ruth, of course, knows no one save Naomi, and the text does not disclose Naomi's memory of her relative Boaz. Boaz's existence comes as a bit of a surprise. After all, Naomi made it clear to her daughters-in-law in 1:12-13 that she had nothing to offer them, and that remaining with her was nothing more than a "dead end" (Streete 1997, 68).

The element of surprise or chance is to be expected in a comedy. The genre turns on these unexpected encounters that move the plot forward. "As luck would have it," Ruth comes to a field that belongs to Boaz. Thanks to the narrator's tip, the reader knows that this man is a relative, which raises the question about the extent to which the encounter is accidental or not. The information is repeated in verse 3: "Boaz, who was of the family of Elimelech." The narrative structure is clearly emphasizing Boaz's identity as a relative. The narrator knows it, and the reader knows it, but the person who just so happens to be gleaning in this man's field does not.

Also of note is the word used here for relative. It is a nominal form derived from the verb (*yada*) "to know." A relative is one who is known. The interest here is in the range of meaning that comes with the verb "to know." This knowing is not simply a cognitive ability, but speaks to familiarity and experience. Knowing someone can refer to meeting someone and it can refer to familiarity, even sexual intimacy. That Boaz is "known" suggests that he is recognized or acknowledged as belonging. The root for this type of knowing carries the possibility that others can come to be experienced and known and therefore recognized or acknowledged as belonging. In a most practical sense, one way an outsider becomes an insider is through marriage and its consummation, which is a way of "knowing."

Ruth's words to Naomi in this first section anticipate something positive, much like the narrator's information at the beginning of the chapter. Ruth hopes to glean "behind someone in whose sight I may find favor." In one sense, Ruth's words may simply refer to her being allowed to glean unmolested, but as the chapter unfolds, she will find so much more than that. The "someone in whose sight" she finds favor is not just anyone. The identity of this "someone" will make the difference in this story.

Theological Analysis

The second chapter begins with the narrator's insider information. The disclosing of this information reinforces the idea that there are multiple voices and perspectives in the narrative. If the narrator knows things that the characters do not, the readers should not assume that we are privy to all of the details. The multiple perspectives are mirrored by the multiple locations in the narrative. The events of the story occur in known places (Boaz's field) and unknown places (somewhere between Moab and Bethlehem). From a theological perspective, events take place in known locations (the realm of the characters) and in unknown places, but not unknown to God. With no one else around, Ruth makes a covenant with Naomi that affirms Ruth's place as Naomi's daughter. Ruth and Naomi make a plan for their survival in 2:2, but in verse one the narrator tips the reader to a possibility that Ruth and Naomi know nothing about. From a literary perspective, this is the stuff of comedy. Our theological lens brings an understanding of these activities as more than a literary device; they are the work of God. Ruth's plan will take her to an unknown place in a foreign land where she will have an encounter with someone who, according to the narrator, is known (a relative). The narrative timing and the characters combined in this location make for a meeting of tremendous significance—it is a theology of surprise.

"JUST THEN, BOAZ CAME..." (2:4-16)

While Ruth gleans, Boaz, Naomi's relative, appears. He greets the reapers and then inquires about Ruth. "To whom does this young woman belong?" he asks (v. 5). The servant tells Boaz about Ruth, and Boaz then addresses Ruth directly, instructing her to glean in his fields and work with his girls. Ruth bows and asks what she has done to garner such favor. Boaz then reveals that he has heard about Ruth and what she has done for Naomi. He blesses her, and she responds by acknowledging his kindness and her unworthiness. At mealtime, Boaz invites Ruth to share in the meal. When she returns to work he tells his workers to pull grain from their stalks and leave it for Ruth to glean.

Literary Analysis

Scholars have long acknowledged the symmetrical structure of the book of Ruth as a whole and within each chapter. Although these readings vary in their detail, a simplified outline of chapter 2 has these elements:

Narrative framework (dialogue between Ruth and Naomi), 2:1-3
Dialogue between Boaz and workers, 2:4-7
Dialogue between Boaz and Ruth, 2:8-13
Boaz commands Ruth, 2:14
Boaz commands workers, 2:15-16
Narrative framework (dialogue between Ruth and Naomi), 2:17-23

This is a highly stylized and carefully crafted narrative, which emphasizes the dialogue between Boaz (the first man to speak in the narrative) and Ruth in the center of the chapter. The section consists of a brief exchange between Boaz and his workers (vv. 4 to 7), followed by two exchanges between Boaz and Ruth (vv. 8-13 and 14), followed by a command to the workers (vv. 15-16).

Also present in this story are the comedic elements of timing and placement that advance the plot. Although they are almost identical in length (chapter 1 has twenty-two verses and chapter 2 has twenty-three) there is a marked temporal difference between chapters 1 and 2. Whereas the narrative action of chapter 1 covers a period of more than 10 years, the majority of the action in chapter 2 takes place within one day. Moving from chapter 1 to chapter 2, the reader experiences a shift in the pace of the narration, directing the reader to focus in on the events of a single day. Although the pace of chapter 2 is much slower, the structure still supports the central encounter.

In addition to the shift in pace, there is a change in setting. The narrative of chapter 1 starts and ends in Bethlehem, but the central action takes place in the plains of Moab, away from home. Similarly, the dialogue between Naomi and Ruth takes place in an undisclosed location on the way to Judah. The unspecified locale of chapter 1 sits in contrast to the specific location for the dialogue of chapter 2. The exchange between Boaz and Ruth takes place in the field of Boaz, and the place where meals are taken is within the sight, if not within the hearing, of others. The temporal and spatial shifts between these chapters signals a movement from general to specific, from private (unknown) to public (known). Ruth's decision to attach herself to Naomi in chapter 1 is a private transaction, located in the margins, but that vow has public implications in the second chapter.

The encounter between Ruth and Boaz in chapter 2 is the narrative moment that moves the story line forward. In a comedy, this encounter functions as a hook in the narrative upon which all subsequent actions hang. In this scene, Boaz and Ruth engage in a very polite conversation. The language is laden with polite terminology and, like his language, Boaz heaps blessings upon Ruth. He refers to her as "my daughter," indicating another shift in identity. Like her title, "my daughter," the invitation to eat with Boaz confirms a shift or elevation in status.

Exegetical Analysis

The coincidence of Ruth arriving in Boaz's field is followed by the surprise arrival of the owner. The text conveys this unexpected event with the word "*hinneh,*" which is translated "behold" or "just then" (NRSV), or "it happened that" or "presently" (*TANAKH*), "Boaz came from Bethlehem" (v. 4). The use of the term "*hinneh*" is not rare. It is a demonstrative or interjection used to connote surprise or get attention. Its rendering as "behold" in the KJV is helpful. "Behold" is visual. Like its counterpart in Hebrew, it calls the reader to "look," allowing something or someone to appear in the narrative just as an object or person would in a field of vision. In this passage where the reader is aware of the narrator, the question is, to whom is the "behold" directed? Is the narrator referring to the surprise of the characters (i.e., the foreman or Ruth) or addressing the reader? Since the *hinneh* clause that introduces Boaz includes the information that he came from Bethlehem, it is likely that the narrator is thinking of the reader—knowing that Boaz just came from Bethlehem helps explain how he might have already heard of Ruth's faithfulness. It is also possible, however, that while the *hinneh* works to alert the reader, it also functions to indicate some suddenness or surprise on the part of the characters.

Boaz's arrival in verse 4 is quickly followed by a dialogue between Boaz and his workers. First, there is the formal greeting, "The LORD be with you," followed by the appropriate response, "The LORD bless you." The greeting is followed by a question. If the reader anticipates that Boaz will inquire about the state of the harvest, there will be another surprise. Boaz's question to his servant goes right to the foreign woman, "To whom does this woman belong?" Boaz's question reflects the narrative's interest, if not his own, in Ruth. The subject of his inquiry raises questions for the reader. Does Ruth stand out so much that she immediately gains Boaz's attention? Or is Boaz the type of person who is aware of all the details of his property? What makes Ruth the center of his concern? Does she look like a foreigner? Does Boaz, like the narrator, have insider information?

Boaz's question is one of identity, but it is identity rooted in a cultural context. One's identity is tied to kin, the people "to whom one belongs." Identity is family, kinship group, and land, and Ruth is impoverished in these areas. Identity and belonging to a people is exacerbated by gender. Women belong to men in the family. In one sense, her location as a reaper reflects her position as someone without a kinship group and the land that accompanies it. On the other hand, the comedic elements of this chapter lend a sense of irony to the question. Ruth is close to the man who will become her husband and provide her with land, family, and a kinship group. In this way, the question of Boaz has more than one answer.

The servant responds to Boaz's inquiry with these words, "She is the Moabite who came back with Naomi from the country of

Moab" (v. 6). The servant's response is redundant: she is the *Moabite* from *Moab* who came back with Naomi. The dual mention of Ruth's Moabite ancestry is parallel with the two references to Boaz's relationship to Naomi: "Naomi had a kinsman on her husband's side ... of the family of Elimelech." Ruth's identifying characteristics are in tension. She is both a Moabite, which makes her other, and with Naomi, which makes her a relative. Which characteristic is more important? The servant's response goes on to include Ruth's words: "Please let me glean and gather among the sheaves behind the reapers." In chapter 1, Ruth asks to cling to a bereft widow who has no visible means. In chapter 2, Ruth asks to glean to salvage that which has been left behind in the field. The servant's answer gives Boaz additional information about who Ruth is. His comments about her work in the fields demonstrate her determination and commitment exhibited in chapter 1. His comments also disclose that Ruth is strong, and physical strength is a desired characteristic for women of child-bearing age. We see this in the story of Abraham's servant who goes out in search of a wife for Isaac. The "test" devised is that the servant will ask for water and the right woman will comply and offer to water his camels—animals that drink quite a bit of water. The test will demonstrate the hospitality of the bride, but also her strength, which will come in handy in a culture where the ability to bear children and survive is of the utmost importance.

Without warning, the narrative shifts quickly from Boaz's dialogue with the harvesters to one with Ruth in verse 8. There is no explanation of Ruth's location prior to these words. Was she close by or did Boaz send for her? The narrative offers no account of an introduction. Rather, the text moves from words of inquiry about Ruth, to words addressed to her. "Now listen, my daughter" (v. 8) are the words that initiate his conversation with Ruth. The servant gave Boaz a few components that would identify Ruth, namely that she was a Moabite and related to Naomi. It is unknown to the reader which of these factors will matter more to Boaz. By addressing her as "my daughter," Boaz immediately places himself in the position of relative and protector. In the same way that Ruth proclaimed to Naomi that she was Naomi's people in the previous chapter, Boaz's use of the title "daughter" for Ruth is performative language that creates a new reality.

The term for daughter is a common one that has a wide range of usage. In addition to referring to a birth daughter, it connotes an adopted daughter, daughter-in-law, sister, half-sister, cousin, granddaughter, in short, it connotes female kin. The word also is used to refer to a people or nation. For example the "daughters of Jerusalem" would be the Israelite women. It is also used to denote a characteristic or quality. In 1 Sam 1:16, Hannah assures Eli that she is not a "worthless woman," literally a "daughter of worthlessness". Ruth has demonstrated that she is a daughter of faithfulness. The range of usage suggests that "daughter" implies a sense of belonging. When Boaz asks, "To whom does this young woman belong" he is effectively asking, whose daughter is she? His salutation, "my daughter," introduces the hope that he will claim her. "Daughter" is a term of endearment, the language of family. When Boaz uses the term "daughter," he counts Ruth among his kin.

Boaz calls Ruth "daughter" with a purpose. Verses 8-9 include seven commands for Ruth: "Now *listen,* my daughter, *do not go* to glean in another field or leave this one, but *keep close* to my young women. *Keep* your eyes on the field that is being reaped, and *follow* behind them. I have ordered the young men not to bother you. If you get thirsty, *go* to the vessels and *drink* from what the young men have drawn" (emphasis added). The commands that Ruth is given are in the context of kinship. As one of his daughters, she will be expected to stay close by, and she will be provided for. Boaz's instructions to Ruth are full of covenant imagery. Boaz's words to Ruth, like Ruth's to Naomi in chapter 1, lay claim to family ties and then name the conditions of the relationship.

Just as we observe in the ancient Near Eastern treaties between the suzerain (lord) and the servants, and with the Ten Commandments, the relationship is first established, and then the expectations that arise out of that are explained. When YHWH said to Israel, "I am the LORD your God" he is reminding Israel of their established relationship, which will require certain behaviors.

Similarly, when Boaz invokes the phrase, "my daughter," he, like YHWH, is saying, "you are mine and I am yours." This is then followed by commands.

Ruth responds to Boaz's words with humility and gratitude. She prostrates herself before him and uses polite, deferential language: "Why have I found favor in your sight, that you should take *notice* of me when I am a *foreigner*?" (v.10, emphasis added). Here we observe a play on words between the terms in italics, "notice" and "foreigner," which both come from the same root, *nacar*, meaning "to recognize, acknowledge, be acquainted with, distinguish and perceive" (Brown, Driver, Briggs, 647-48). Boaz *notices* Ruth, which leads to his inquiry of her and then he *acknowledges* her by calling her "daughter." These two terms from the same root signal a progression from simply seeing to perceiving. The wordplay suggests he acknowledges her. This recognition stands in contrast to the fact that she is a foreigner or other. Ruth's question to Boaz presses him to explain how it is that he extends this kindness to her.

Boaz's response reveals that he already knows about Ruth. "All that you have done for your mother-in-law since the death of husband has been fully told me" (v. 11). Here is confirmed what the reader expected. The initial questions about Ruth's identity were intentional. Boaz wasn't asking who the stranger was; he was trying to identify Ruth. What appears in the comedy to be coincidental is quite intentional. Although she is an outsider to those in the fields, she is already known to Boaz.

In the same way that the narrator knows something about Boaz's identity that Ruth did not, so too Boaz knew something of Ruth's identity. Boaz heard of what Ruth had done for Naomi, and for Boaz these acts are the identifying markers. It is noteworthy that the positive evaluation of Ruth comes not from the narrator but from Boaz. Here the text uses the words of the characters within the narrative to affirm what the reader who is outside of the narrative has already gleaned from chapter 1, namely that Ruth is faithful and her faithfulness is apparent to everyone.

His account of what Ruth has done, forsaking her mother and father and the land of her birth, coming to a people she did not know, once again evokes the journey of Abraham. Boaz offers a blessing upon her deeds, namely a "full recompense," one of completeness and satisfaction. This blessing is offered against the backdrop of the harvest, signaling more than an end to the famine. The deferential and formal language slows down the narrative action even more and draws attention to itself, raising the question, what is the purpose of this elaborate language? Is there something else going on behind this dialogue?

We should not overlook the possibility that this elaborate, polite exchange is a thin veil over attraction on the part of either Boaz or Ruth, or both. Boaz may have noticed Ruth for reasons other than her virtuous acts. Ruth's response could be motivated by more than gratitude.

Boaz's blessing includes reference to YHWH's "wings," under which Ruth has "come for refuge" (v. 12). This term connotes an image of YHWH's protective covering and is also used to apply to cloaks and garments. Perhaps Boaz is indicating to Ruth that he is willing to offer her protection. Ruth's deferential response contains a request that she "continue to find favor in his sight," as he has "spoken to the heart" of his "servant," even though she is "not one of your servants" (v. 13, author's translation). Her words acknowledge her sense of unworthiness and possibly suggest that she is not another servant. The words strain as they cover the possibility of polite speech and the language of courtship, all the while conveying the social reality that these two people occupy different positions in society.

In verse 14, Boaz invites her to a meal and again the text conveys abundance. The delicacy of parched grain was "heaped up" for her. She was "satisfied" and there were leftovers. This image of abundance stands in contrast to Ruth's past experiences of famine and death. It also stands in contradiction to her current state as a widow who is forced to glean. When she returns to work in verse 15, Boaz authorizes additional grain to be left for her so that she gleaned an ephah, 29–50 U.S. pounds, which would have been enough for several weeks. In just one day, there is an abundance of grain, blessing and words that signal an end to the years of famine and loss.

As noted in the previous section, the dialogue dominates this section. Boaz speaks with his workers and then with Ruth. It is through the dialogue that we determine what Boaz thinks of Ruth. When he calls her "my daughter," he evokes Naomi's designation for Ruth in this same chapter (v. 2). Both Naomi and Boaz call her "daughter," suggesting that both acknowledge a connection, a family bond of some sort. The fact that they both call her "daughter" raises the question of how that will become manifest in Boaz's relationship with Ruth.

Of particular importance in this second chapter are the elements of timing and placement. Ruth and Boaz find themselves in the same place at the same time. From a literary perspective, this is the timing of a comedy. The placement of Boaz and Ruth also points to the intentional structure in the book. It is the second major encounter in the narrative thus far. In chapter 1, Ruth and Naomi have an encounter where Ruth demands to remain in Naomi's family. Whether her motivation is duty or love or both, it speaks to her faithfulness. In this second chapter, Ruth has an encounter with Boaz, where she is deferential as Boaz calls her "my daughter" and makes reference to YHWH's wings as a place where she can trust. The first encounter is private and the second public, but in each, the elements of recognition/nonrecognition are present. In chapter 1, Ruth's identity shifted from one in covenant with Mahlon to someone in covenant with Naomi. In chapter 2, her identity shifts from "the Moabitess from Moab" to "my daughter."

As stated earlier, the root of the adjective for foreigner, *nacri*, comes from the verb *nacar*, meaning to "regard, recognize." It also has usage as "be willing to recognize or acknowledge, be acquainted with, distinguish, or understand" (Brown, Driver, Briggs, 648). Clearly, this term means not simply to "see" but to "perceive"; to make a judgment call. The way one is designated an outsider is by "distinguishing" between one set of practices, values, or characteristics and another. Similarly, the way one is considered family will call upon the same verb, and here the challenge will be to "acknowledge." When Boaz gives report of what Ruth has done, he is "acknowledging" her faithfulness. When he calls her "my daughter," he acknowledges her unique status, "distinguishing" her, not in an attempt to exclude her from Israel, but perhaps to exclude her from other foreigners so that he can bring her into his own family.

As his "daughter" Ruth is given a series of commands in verses 8 and 9: "do not go to glean in another field or leave this one," "keep close [cling] to my young women," "keep your eyes on the field that is being reaped," and "follow behind them." The reference to "clinging" supports Ruth's embodiment of *hesed*. Boaz instructs her to "cling" to his young women in verse 8. In verse 9 his instruction continues and he tells her to "walk" or "follow behind" his young women, evoking Ruth's entreaty to Naomi in 1:16 not to keep her from returning "after" her. Verses 8-9, with their references to Boaz's women and men, reflect Boaz's inclusion of her, which depends upon Ruth's clinging. If Ruth clings to Boaz's people, there is provision. Verse 14 goes further in suggesting that if Ruth clings to Boaz himself, there is ample provision—more than she needs—and this abundance stands in stark contrast to the famine, barrenness, and death of chapter 1.

The eating scene evokes abundance and alludes to other encounters that suggest marriage. In verse 9, Boaz instructs Ruth to "drink from what the young men have drawn." This reference to drawn water evokes the motif of the well meeting. Abraham's servant encountered Rebekah at a well and Jacob met Rachel at a well as did Moses and Zipporah. The word for "drawing" the water also connotes "attract."

Boaz gives instructions to his young men regarding Ruth in verses 15 and 16. They are told to allow her access to the standing sheaves and "do not reproach her." Ordinarily, gleaners would not be permitted near the standing sheaves. Moreover, the young men are told to pull out grain from the gathered barley for her and not to rebuke her. These instructions form a reversal. As a gleaner, Ruth is beneath the harvesters, yet they are commanded to give her special treatment. Here we see further examples of the way identity is constructed. Before Boaz's arrival, Ruth was a Moabite and a lone woman who was vulnerable to abuse. Now, after Boaz's encounter with Ruth, she is a part of his family, someone who deserves special treatment. Ruth's location hasn't changed, but her encounter with Boaz and his recognition of her results in changes to her identity.

Twice now (in chapters 1 and 2), Ruth has an encounter with a member of Elimelech's family in an attempt to establish her identity, and identity is connected to recognition. When we encounter another person, what do we recognize in the other and on what basis do we determine who belongs and who doesn't? This moment of recognition/nonrecognition is central to the narrative. Behind Boaz's question, "To whom does this young woman belong?" are a multitude of other questions. When I see you, can I recognize you or identify something that makes you familiar? Can Boaz recognize in Ruth those characteristics that make her family?

In chapter 2, the one characteristic that Boaz identifies in Ruth is her faithfulness. Ruth's *hesed* is the characteristic for which he knows her. Just as God's *hesed* consistently bridges the gap between God and God's people, so too will Ruth's faithfulness cover the gap created between herself and Naomi because of Mahlon's death. In chapter 2, this faithfulness will bridge the separation between an Israelite landowner and a foreign gleaner.

Theological Analysis

What is interesting about this godly plan is that it involves a Moabite. On the narrative level, Ruth is the Moabite widow. That makes her the spoiler, the baggage, the other. On a theological level, it is this outsider who is the agent for change in the narrative. The Moabite widow is the link between Naomi and Boaz. She is the one who, along with Boaz, will bring new life to Naomi and it is she who literally and figuratively bears the seed home to Naomi. Ruth's faithfulness to Naomi allows her to demonstrate the faithfulness of God to a people who are barren. In the same sense that the widowed Naomi is a "dead end" for Ruth and Orpah, so too Israel has nothing of value to offer YHWH, but it is YHWH's faithfulness to an undeserving nation that brings new life into what was once dead.

In chapter 1, we observed that the covenant God made with Israel functioned like a *ketubbah,* or marriage contract, which meant that God married an undeserving bride. In chapter 2, Boaz's designation of Ruth as daughter declares that God has not only adopted someone who is undesirable, but that the adopted child has been given a place of honor, just as Ruth was given status among Boaz's workers. This inclusion in God's family is made on the basis of Ruth's faithfulness. It is the reason Boaz reaches out to Ruth, and it is the way that Israel can stay in right relationship with God.

Moreover, the narrative makes the theological assertion that God can and will move wherever and with whomever God chooses. The constructs of identity that limit the characters in the narrative are not limiting to God. In this way, Ruth is the embodiment of *hesed.* By going out and gleaning, she forms the connection between Naomi and Boaz, who both call her daughter. She brings grain from Boaz's field to Naomi, who was empty, and she secures the family recognition on behalf of Naomi. In the same way that YHWH's faithfulness is not dependent upon the worthiness or likelihood of the recipient, Ruth's faithfulness benefits a childless widow, one of the "least of these" in this society. Moreover, by virtue of her own status as outsider/other, her embodiment of *hesed* challenges our assumptions about who merits God's mercy—in short, no one does. God's relationship with Israel results from God's faithfulness and God's desire to be with Israel, just as Ruth's desire to be with Naomi and her faithfulness make her a bridge that connects Naomi and Boaz to a new future.

Both Boaz and Ruth reflect characteristics of God. Ruth demonstrates God's faithfulness through her faithfulness to Naomi. Boaz demonstrates God's faithfulness in providing abundantly for those who are in need. Both demonstrate aspects of God's *hesed* to God's people, and if that is the case, chapter 2 suggests that Boaz's providing for Ruth means the definition of God's people is broader than perhaps Israel originally thought.

Not only does the God of Israel use outsiders in this narrative. We also observe that the work of God begins in unofficial or outside places. Boaz identifies Ruth as "daughter" but he is not the first to do so; Naomi did in chapter 1:11-13. In this sense, Boaz is confirming or making official what was already done by a widow and a Moabite somewhere between Moab and Bethlehem—"no-man's-land." Once again, the audience has insider information, or a preview to the ensuing action. This narrative contains coexisting stories, "counter-narratives." Often we will find the work of God in these "other" stories. Ruth reminds us to pay attention to the parts of the story that take place in the margins and the center, in known and unknown locations.

In different locations, the characters must find and see and recognize one another anew. In Ruth, these encounters demand that the characters see or recognize differently. We sometimes have difficulty recognizing people we know in different contexts. For example, children often experience a moment of cognitive dissonance when they encounter their schoolteachers in a context other than that of the classroom. In that moment the student must acknowledge that the teacher does not live at the school and, in fact, has a life outside of the school. This means that sometimes we don't immediately recognize people we know because we encounter them in places where we didn't expect to see them. This is why Jacob expresses surprise in Gen 28:16, when he encountered God at Bethel, "Surely the LORD is in this place—and I did not know it!" It never occurred to him that he would encounter God when on the run from his brother. Similarly, in Ruth, the Israelites have expectations about Moabites, and when Ruth shows up in unexpected places exhibiting behavior that is unexpected for a Moabite, the Israelites have a moment of nonrecognition before the moment of recognition. Each time the characters have encounters in different locations, they have to navigate what they know about the other in one context in a new environment. In the encounter in chapter 2, Boaz identifies characteristics of Ruth that had not been recognized in other contexts.

"WHERE DID YOU GLEAN TODAY?" (2:19-23)

Ruth's gleaning on that first day yields about two-thirds of a bushel (an ephah), which is quite a bit for one day's gleaning. She carries the grain to Naomi and shares with her. Naomi inquires about where Ruth gleaned and when Ruth answered Boaz, Naomi tells her that he is a relative. Ruth then tells Naomi of Boaz's instructions to stay close to his servants. Naomi approves of this idea and Ruth continues to glean in Boaz's fields until the end of the barley and wheat harvests.

Literary Analysis

What begins as a "chance" encounter at the beginning of this chapter concludes with a wealthy relative, more than enough grain, and the promise of sustenance for the near future. The resolution at the end of the chapter offers the reader a hope for a resolution that will last for even longer. This second chapter moves forward by the disclosing of information. First, the narrator gives information to the reader. Then Boaz requires information to identify Ruth, but we quickly learn he has information about her identity that he discloses to her when she asks how she has garnered his favor. In this final segment, Naomi asks questions of Ruth and Ruth's answers bring hope to the widow Naomi and her daughter-in-law. Naomi's words not only confirm what Ruth learned, they assure her that Boaz is, in fact, a good relative.

Exegetical Analysis

The chapter concludes with Ruth's return to Naomi, bringing closure to the narrative that started with the search for food. She returns at the end of the chapter with food in abundance. Naomi's words, "Where did you glean today? And where have you worked? Blessed be the man who took notice of you" (v. 19) introduce through dialogue the elements of recognition/nonrecognition again. Boaz sees and inquires about Ruth, followed by an encounter between the two. In their exchange it becomes clear that Boaz already knew about Ruth, just as the reader already knew about Boaz. Boaz's overt graciousness toward Ruth allows for more than just grain from gleaning. When she returns home with a report for Naomi, Naomi remembers Boaz and recognizes the potential for immediate and perhaps long-term provision.

The surprise or chance encounter is mitigated by the narrator's introductory words. It is an unexpected meeting for Ruth, but it is not a chance encounter. In the narrative structure, the meeting was predetermined; these two had to meet. The seemingly accidental circumstances under which Boaz and Ruth come together within the narrative suggest a structure that wants to make this encounter a pivotal event in the narrative. In fact, this encounter uses all the aforementioned motifs of meeting/parting, loss/acquisition, search/discovery, and recognition/nonrecognition. First, Boaz notices Ruth as someone he doesn't know and then the inquiry begins. He subsequently acknowledges her as a member of his family. This second recognition is another turning point in the narrative. This dialogue, first about Ruth and then with Ruth, is what enacts the change in the second chapter. In the same way that the dialogue of covenant between Naomi and Ruth makes them family, so Boaz's recognition of Ruth as daughter sets a course of action that eventually leads to the resolution of the crisis of death, famine, and eventually childlessness. For the time being, the recognition of Ruth by Boaz means that the widows will have food through the end of the barley harvest. Chapter 1 ends with the temporal notation that the barley harvest has begun. Chapter 2 concludes with the end of the barley and wheat harvests.

With a return to the narrative action (v. 17), Ruth goes back to the work of gleaning and produces an ephah of barley (approximately 10–20 liters or two-thirds of a bushel). She takes the barley back to the city and provides for her mother-in-law out of this abundance (or her fullness). Another reversal presents itself in this verse. Ruth left on this first day to glean, the work of gathering leftovers. At the conclusion of the chapter, she returns with a substantial amount. Thus to the Naomi who left full and returned empty, Ruth goes out empty and returns full. Ruth tells Naomi all that happened that day, ending with the name of the man, Boaz, which gives Naomi cause to praise YHWH "whose kindness/*hesed* has not forsaken the living or the dead!" (v. 20). Naomi's words evoke her earlier statement to her daughters-in-law in 1:8, "May the LORD deal kindly/*hesed* with you, as you have dealt with the dead and with me." In chapter 1, Naomi's hope is that YHWH will show *hesed* to her daughters-in-law as they have to her, and in chapter 2, she praised YHWH, whose *hesed* has been demonstrated through the actions of Ruth and Boaz. In each blessing, the faithfulness of YHWH is affirmed as something that extends beyond the living to the dead. Naomi's understanding of YHWH's faithfulness is limited by her own perception. In chapter 1, she wanted to send her daughters-in-law away because she had nothing to offer them. In chapter 2 we observe that it is through her daughter-in-law, Ruth, that YHWH will demonstrate faithfulness to Naomi.

Naomi comments on the inherent safety afforded Ruth by staying close (clinging) to Boaz's workers (vv. 22-25). In chapter 1, Ruth clung to Naomi and became her kin. In this chapter, Ruth has been instructed to cling to the servants of Boaz, as a sign of being his kin. The final verse of the chapter has Ruth living with Naomi and clinging to Boaz's young women through the barley and wheat harvest (April–May).

Theological Analysis

Naomi responds to Ruth's good report with a blessing: "Blessed be he by the LORD, whose kindness has not forsaken the living or the dead!" (v. 20). This blessing of Boaz in his faithfulness is rooted in the faithfulness of the Lord. In contrast to Naomi's words upon their return to Bethlehem, she now acknowledges God's faithfulness to the living and the dead. It is not the case that Naomi's earlier words that describe God as the cause of her bitterness were untrue; they were simply the words of her experience at that time. Like all laments, they cry out about what is wrong in the hope that God will intervene. After the extended period of loss in chapter 1, the trajectory of the story is changed in one day by the faithfulness of one man in response to the faithfulness of one woman.

Naomi's blessing acknowledges that God's faithfulness has not failed the living or the dead. This brings to mind the reference to the living and the dead in chapter 1, where Naomi praises her daughters-in-law for their faithfulness to the deceased and to her. The repetition reminds the reader of a cultural identity that extends beyond death. A theological lens recognizes the faithfulness of God as something that is not limited by famine or geography or death. Israel can look for the faithfulness of God under any set of circumstances.

Naomi's identity has changed dramatically. She is without husband and sons and any real external security. Yet here she is able to acknowledge God's faithfulness. Naomi's words of praise speak to the possibility of reclaiming an identity on the other side of her exile in Moab. This identity is rooted in the faithfulness of YHWH.

CHAPTER 3
A CLOAKED COVENANT

Almost all of chapter 3 is direct speech. There is an exchange between Naomi and Ruth regarding a plan of action. The executed plan results in a dialogue between Boaz and Ruth and the chapter concludes with a conversation between the two women that interprets the action. All of the dialogue surrounds the action in verses 6-8, namely Ruth's encounter with Boaz on the threshing floor.

"I NEED TO SEEK SOME SECURITY FOR YOU ..." (3:1-5)

Naomi has a plan. She instructs Ruth to go to the threshing floor at night where Boaz will be that evening. Ruth is to "make herself presentable," go unobserved to the threshing floor, and keep an eye on Boaz, taking care to note his sleeping place. Once he is asleep, Ruth is to go to his sleeping place, uncover his "feet," lay there, and await his instructions. Ruth consents.

Literary Analysis

Like those that precede it, the third chapter has three sections. Verses 1-5 and 16-18 are conversations between Naomi and Ruth. Between these dialogic bookends is an encounter between Ruth and Boaz in verses 6-15. This pattern of words framing the action in chapters 2 and 3 is in contrast to chapter 1, where the action surrounds the dialogue. The dialogue between Ruth and Naomi was central in chapter 1. In chapters 2 and 3, the dialogue between the two women provides the lens through which we can observe what happens in the center of the chapter. If dialogue bridges the gap between insider and outsider and transforms identity, then the conversations surrounding the encounters in chapters 2 and 3 are critical for Ruth's new identity. The themes of concealing and revealing, covering and uncovering are central to the establishment of identity.

Exegetical Analysis

Whereas chapter 2 begins with Ruth making plans for her and Naomi's immediate needs, chapter 3 begins with Naomi making plans for their long-term future. Naomi speaks with authority in these first five verses and she does most of the talking. She knows Boaz's activities for the night. The instructions she gives to Ruth are like that of the narrator in chapter 2. Naomi's instructions dominate this section and serve as literary foreshadowing. They direct the reader to anticipate an encounter that will resolve the tensions in the narrative. Ruth responds with a few words, namely, "all that you tell me I will do" (v. 5). In addition to being obedient, Ruth's few words suggest a shift in power of sorts. Up until this point in the narrative, Ruth has not been at a loss for words. When Naomi ordered Ruth to return home in chapter 1, Ruth resisted until Naomi had nothing else to say. In chapter 2, Ruth did not lack vocabulary for her exchange with Boaz. In chapter 3, Ruth's few words convey obedience to Naomi, but her obedience will require that she take a risk.

In verse 1, she addresses Ruth with a familial term, "my daughter." This is the term Boaz uses at the end of chapter 2. Both Boaz and Naomi assert some relationship with Ruth before issuing their instructions. Naomi goes on to say, "I need to seek some security for you, so that it may be well with you." Since Naomi is bound to Ruth, securing her daughter-in-law's future means she is securing her own. As was the case in chapter 2 where Boaz seems to know things about Ruth, here in chapter 3, Naomi has conducted surveillance and knows that the winnowing of the barley will happen and that Boaz will be there. Naomi's instructions are supported by a string of verbs, beginning with "wash," "anoint," and "put on" (a cloak or mantle). The preparation alerts us that this is no ordinary encounter. Ruth's appearance here does matter. Do Naomi's instructions direct Ruth to make sure she is sexually attractive or is she telling Ruth to remove her widow's attire, or both? The changing of clothes and the encounter with a potential husband/*levir* evokes the Tamar story in Gen 38.

The story of Tamar and Judah interrupts the Joseph narrative. After Joseph is sold into slavery and Jacob mourns the loss of his beloved son in chapter 37, the text abruptly shifts its focus onto Judah, Jacob's fourth-born, who suggested the brothers sell Joseph to the Ishmaelites as a slave. Judah marries a Canaanite woman and has three sons, Er, Onan, and Shelah. He then secures Tamar as a wife for his firstborn son, Er. Unfortunately, Er "was wicked in the sight of the LORD, and the LORD put him to death" (Gen 38:7). The narrative dispatches Er swiftly and deftly. Tamar is given to the second-born, Onan, as a wife so that Onan can "perform the duty of a brother-in-law" or l*evir* for her (Gen 38:8). Onan, reluctant to share in the inheritance, employed coitus interruptus to prevent Tamar from conceiving, which "was displeasing in the sight of the LORD, and he put him to death also" (Gen 38:10). Tamar is sent back to her father's house to wait for the third son, Shelah, to grow up, but Judah is duplicitous. The text informs us his instructions were motivated by his fear "that he [Shelah] too would die, like his brothers" (Gen 38:11).

After some time passes, Judah's wife dies. Shelah grows up and Tamar realizes that she has not been given to Shelah as a wife. In response to her perception, she removes her widow's clothing and dons a veil. She then sits down at the entrance to Enaim. Judah, on his way to sheepshearing in Timnah, sees a woman he assumes to be a prostitute. He negotiates a pledge for an encounter with the woman. As a result of their tryst, the woman conceives. Some time passes when it is discovered that Tamar is pregnant. Judah quickly pronounces the sentence to burn her. As Tamar was brought out, she produces Judah's personal belongings, his identifying markers, and names him as the father. Judah acknowledges his items and pronounces, "She is more in the right than I, since I did not give her to my son Shelah" (Gen 38:26). In due time, Tamar gives birth to twin sons, Perez and Zerah.

There are a number of similarities between the story of Tamar and that of Ruth. Both Tamar and Ruth are widows in need of an heir. Like the sons of Naomi and Elimelech, the names of the sons are suggestive. "Er is a possible wordplay on "evil,"" Onan forms a sound pair with the word for "sorrow, trouble or wickedness," and Shelah can mean "something asked for" (Hendel 2006, 62). In both narratives, the women take the offensive and thereby gain an advantage. In both, the allure of female sexuality is employed to obtain the security of preserving the family line. Also, in both, the identity of the woman is in question. In Gen 38, Tamar wears a veil that causes Judah to mistake her for a prostitute. She allows him to do so in order to achieve her goal. In this account, Ruth has at least two covers. She covers herself with clothes and she goes to Boaz under the cover of darkness.

Unlike Judah in Gen 38, Boaz asks the woman who she is. She discloses her identity and requests his protection. A comparison of these two passages results in a positive depiction of Boaz. He is a good kinsman, a likely redeemer. Although Ruth employs stealth to gain a private audience with Boaz, he is willing to help Ruth. Unlike his ancestor Judah, he does not have to be shamed into the right action.

In the first set of verbs, Naomi commands Ruth to clean up and put on her clothes, in this instance a cloak (v. 3). The term used here for cloak, "*simlah*," connotes an "outer garment, usually a square piece of cloth worn as an outer garment, cloak or mantle" sometimes a "covering in sleep...bed covering" (Brown, Driver, and Briggs 2001, 971). In the Ruth narrative, it can be seen as an outer garment of protection or as a means of concealing identity, or both. The fact that the *simlah* can also be a bed covering reminds the reader that Ruth's mission is to secure a husband. That she wears a covering and will then uncover Boaz, asking for his covering, supports the theme of revealing/concealing in this passage. Finally, the cloak evokes the possibility of a chuppah, or a marriage canopy.

The next set of verbs is "go down," "do not reveal," and "observe." The plan must be executed at a specific time and place. Ruth will go down to Boaz at night at the end of the harvest. The place is one of harvesting and possibly other unknown activities. Here Naomi instructs Ruth to go down to the place where Boaz and others will be. She is to go unobserved, but to be an observer. She will locate and watch Boaz until he falls asleep on the ground. The command "not to reveal" herself to anyone is literally, "do not make yourself known to anyone." Here the verb for making oneself known is the verb *yada,* which is "to know." Ruth is to go unrecognized by anyone, literally "to a man," all the while observing, or "knowing," Boaz's behaviors (she is to wait until he has finished eating and drinking), and his location, "observe (*know*) where he lies." The obvious wordplay comes from the usage of *yada* for sexual intimacy. Naomi calls Boaz "our kinsman," which literally means one "known to us," connoting familiarity or closeness that results from the family bond. It is interesting that this particular word is used because of the possibilities that come from *yada.* Moreover, Naomi uses the possessive pronoun "our" to modify the kinsman, which affirms Ruth's place in the family. The wordplay here with *yada* suggests that knowing someone or being known by someone is based on the revealing or uncovering, making oneself known to another. This kind of knowing implies some type of vulnerability.

The final set of verbs in Naomi's instructions includes "go," "uncover," and "lie down." This uncovering or revealing of Boaz's feet sets the stage for Ruth to uncover or reveal herself and her intentions to Boaz. All three sets of commands contain a reference to revealing/concealing or recognition/nonrecognition. One question is what exactly is Naomi instructing Ruth to do? Is she to uncover his "feet", a euphemism for his genitals, and lie down? Uncover the place by his "feet" and lie down? Or uncover herself and lie down at his "feet"? It is likely that the narrator is intentionally ambiguous here, exploiting the mysterious and provocative nature of the evening's events.

Of note is the text/critical issue or literary issue of confused pronouns in 3:3-4 in the Hebrew text. The context makes it clear that

Naomi is instructing Ruth, but the pronouns in the narrative are confusing. The text reads, "Now wash and anoint yourself, and put on your best clothes and *I* will go down to the threshing-floor; but do not make yourself known to the man until he has finished eating and drinking. When he lies down, observe the place where he lies; then go and uncover his feet and *I* will lie down; and he will tell you what to do." The written text shifts subjects from second person to first person, from Ruth to Naomi, which raises the question, who is doing what? One solution that is offered is a linguistic one, which argues that the text uses an old form of the second person that looks like a first-person singular. This argument concludes that all the pronouns refer to Ruth. Naomi is instructing Ruth to do these things on the threshing floor, using an older form of language. English translations follow this suggestion that eliminates confusion with the pronouns. While this reading removes the problem, a literary reading sees in the textual problem another possibility. Perhaps the confusion between the two women is intended to remind the reader of another story that has a similar structure, namely that of the origins of Ammon and Moab in Gen 19.

The structure of the narrative that recounts the Moabites' beginnings is the same in Ruth 3. The destruction of Sodom forces Lot to leave behind his land and his wife. He and his daughters take refuge in the caves outside of Zoar. His daughters realized that their family line was threatened with extinction unless they did something. The daughters conspired to get their father drunk and conceive by him. They are both successful and name their sons "Moab," meaning "from my father," and "Ben-ammi," which means "son of my people."

In both texts, the following elements are present: first, there are two women conspiring to continue the family line. Second, there is one man, presumably unsuspecting. Third, there is drinking and darkness involved. Fourth, the central action occurs outside of the cities in liminal space. Fifth, there is uncertainty around the identity of the women and the time of their arrival and departure (this is a commentary on the state of the man or the ability to see). Sixth, children come of these unions. The comparison of Ruth 3 to Gen 19 has the potential to shed light on the role of Naomi in the passage. In Gen 19, both daughters have relations with their father. This is not the case in Ruth 3. Only the Moabite goes down to the threshing floor, but she does so for both women. They act as one and the marriage of Ruth to Boaz is for the protection of both women.

The dialogue between these two stories revisits the tragic story of Gen 19. The story of Ruth and Naomi's plan to secure the line via Boaz has a different outcome. In this story, Moab finds a way back into Israel instead of being led out. Here the Moabite becomes an ancestress to be revered instead of one relegated to shame. Because structural similarities are present and the Moabite line factors into both stories, Harold Fisch argues that the story of Ruth reaches back and redeems the story of Lot's daughters in the same way that Boaz's decision to marry Ruth redeems the line that would have died (Fisch, 435).

The literary structure of Ruth is intentionally linked to Ruth's ancestors (Lot and his daughters) and Boaz's ancestors (Judah and Tamar). In both narratives, a woman (or women) employs some type of "trickery" that positions an unsuspecting man into the role of *levir*. Ruth's contribution to the pattern is the intentional focus on redemption, which allows us to observe not only the redemption of Mahlon and Elimelech's line but also that of Judah, Lot, Moab, and Ammon. The structural similarity between Gen 19:30-38 and Ruth 3:1-5 signals that Moab comes back to Israel in the same way that Moab became an outsider.

Theological Analysis

Chapter 3 opens with Naomi seeking well-being for her Moabite daughter-in-law, who is by definition an outsider. From this comedic challenge comes the theological message that when Naomi seeks well-being for the outsider, she not only challenges the status quo, she also secures a future for herself.

The structural similarities to Gen 38 and Gen 19 remind us that dialogue has a theological payoff. The dialogue between Ruth's story and that of Tamar and Judah and Lot and his daughters demonstrates the "retelling" of a story that allows for new theological truths to be discovered. Specifically, "retelling" a story reminds us that knowing or revelation comes in installments. We learn about Lot and his daughters and Judah and Tamar when we become acquainted with Ruth's story.

The uses of the verb "to know" (*yada*) in verses 2, 3, and 4 connote revelation. Boaz is a relative, which means he is "known" or familiar. Ruth will not disclose her identity to anyone but Boaz once she takes note ("to know") of his location whereupon she will present herself to him in a manner he has not known. This term, "to know," in particular, exploits the possibilities of covenant language as it speaks to the intimacy of covenant and marriage. One refrain throughout the legal and prophetic material, "that they may *know* that I am YHWH," expresses God's desire to be known by God's people.

Ruth's preparation to meet Boaz makes sense on a practical level. It is a good idea to be at one's best when asking to be redeemed. The ritual of washing, anointing, and dressing evokes the consecration of Israel in preparation for their encounter with YHWH at Sinai in Ex 19. The act of consecration acknowledged the holiness of the God Israel served. God's people prepared for the encounter and then awaited the moment of recognition—one of knowing and being known.

"IT MUST NOT BE KNOWN THAT THE WOMAN CAME TO THE THRESHING-FLOOR" (3:6-18)

In the next unit of chapter 3, Ruth follows Naomi's directions and things go according to plan for the most part. Ruth goes stealthily and observes Boaz's sleeping place. She uncovers his feet and lies down. He is awakened in the middle of the night to find a woman at his feet. He asks who she is and Ruth tells him, "I am Ruth, your servant; spread your cloak over your servant [handmaid], for you are next-of-kin" (v. 9). Boaz blesses Ruth for her loyalty. He then tells her that there is a relative who has the right of refusal as redeemer/kinsman. He tells her to stay for the night and he will resolve the issue in the morning. Ruth rises before dawn in order to be undetected, but before she leaves, Boaz gives her six measures of barley to take home.

Literary Analysis

The narrative makes it clear that Boaz's actions coincide with Naomi's plan. Naomi appears to be all-knowing, like the narrator, at least when it comes to Boaz's behavior. Then Ruth's initial actions coincide with Naomi's instructions. At the end of verse 7, the narrative has reached the end of what Naomi's words described. With the same deftness we observed in the first verses in chapter 1, the narrative takes us to midnight. For reasons unbeknownst to the reader (perhaps not to Ruth) Boaz is startled at midnight, turned over, "and there, lying at his feet, was a woman!" (v. 8). Now the reader and Ruth are without Naomi's words to direct the ensuing action. If a comedy constantly overturns reality to reveal that it is only an illusion, then this narrative is true to this form. Naomi's instructions are based on what she knows of Boaz and the context of the threshing floor, but the surprise that awakens Boaz is not a part of the plan. It is a literary surprise, reminding the reader that the power of the story is in the unknown and the unfamiliar. Ruth, along with the narrative, will demand the audience to go beyond the comfort zone of what we recognize.

This encounter is the central moment in the chapter, and as such, location, dialogue, and identity converge so that Boaz is positioned to take on the role of redeemer or next of kin. The moment is serendipitous—the right people are in the right place at the right time and what ensues is initiated by the mysterious "startling" of Boaz. Ruth takes the initiative here, making a request, which moves the narrative toward resolution.

Indeed, all the dialogue in the chapter is about the encounter between Ruth and Boaz in verses 6-8. The dialogue in verse 9 begins with a question. "Who are you?" This question has a literal and symbolic meaning. Boaz asks the question for very real and practical reasons, but on a literary level, the question presents Ruth with an opportunity to name herself. Up until this point, she has been identified by her husband, her mother-in-law, her geographic location, or the people around her. Here, she names/identifies herself both by her name and then as Boaz's handmaid.

Ruth's response has two parts. Her self-identification is followed by a request: "spread our cloak over your servant, for you are next-of-kin." Just as Naomi and Boaz preface their instructions to Ruth with a relational address, so too does Ruth identify herself as "servant" and then make a request of Boaz as "next-of-kin." Ruth's speech does not venture to identify herself as relative, only as servant. Boaz as potential *levir* (a male relative who can inherit on behalf of the widow) will determine whether or not Ruth will officially become kin.

Exegetical Analysis

The central action of this chapter takes place at night at the threshing floor. The activity there involves threshing, winnowing, and sifting the grain, the last step in the harvesting process. Because of the harvest of grain, the threshing floor comes to be associated with fertility within the larger, religious cosmology of the ancient Near East. It is also the location for harvest celebrations and fertility rites. In fact, the word "threshing" is a metaphor for sexual intercourse in many agricultural societies (Streete 1997, 69). The prophet Hosea refers to unseemly behavior, the "whoring of Israel," on the threshing floor (9:1).

The location, setting, and characters converge to create a scene that is fraught with sexuality. The threshing floor is a place associated with fertility, and as noted earlier, the word for feet, *"raglim,"* is a euphemism for genitals (a noted example is 2 Sam 11:8-11), making Ruth's act a bold one. The sexuality in this passage, like most in biblical narrative, is connected to fertility. The grain and the harvest allude to reproduction of all kinds and the future of Elimelech's line is at stake. Children are like grain/food in that they enable a people to survive.

Ruth's trip to the threshing floor is directed by a clear motive—that of security for herself, Naomi, and future generations. What is not clear is why Boaz would spend the night there. He is too important to serve as watchman over the grain. What may not make historical sense makes narrative sense. The process of threshing the grain does not require his presence overnight, but Naomi's plan does, so the narrative places the redeemer/kinsman where he needs to be and when he needs to be there.

What is of interest in this passage is the degree to which time and space (location) operate together to influence and shape identity. In other words, in this chapter, it is not only Boaz's location, but the time Ruth encounters him in this place that influences the outcome of events. The critical action of the narrative takes place in the dark. Ruth is covered both by garments and by darkness following Naomi's instructions not to make herself known, for the purpose of uncovering or making herself vulnerable to Boaz. From a literary perspective the night is both a temporal marker and a literary covering. It locates the events within the chronological narrative, and it heightens a sense of suspense as the reader waits to see what will transpire.

The darkness creates a type of vulnerability for the characters. With limited vision, they must rely on other senses to navigate their surroundings. The limitations of the darkness also offer the opportunity for new revelations.

In the darkness, there is fluidity to Ruth's identity. Naomi instructs her, "Do not make yourself known to the man." She is to remain anonymous to everyone except Boaz, at the right time. It is not Ruth's appearance but her words that will make her recognizable to Boaz. She will make herself known to him, which is different from her identity simply being assigned to her in light of being a Moabite in Judah. Boaz will encounter Ruth in the dark without the ability to recognize her visually. He will be invited to recognize her or "see" her without the traditional identity construct of "other." Under the cover of darkness, Ruth will reveal or make herself known to Boaz through her words and actions. Dialogue will allow Ruth to claim a new identity.

Boaz's vulnerability is conveyed through his uncovering and through the "startling" that occurs at midnight. It is not clear what startles Boaz in his sleep. His "shuddering" could very well be a response to his exposure after having been uncovered, or due to a night wind. It is possible that he had a disturbing dream.

COMMENTARY

Another possibility would be a night demon. Mesopotamian folk-lore and Sumerian myth attest to female demons that threaten men sleeping alone (Fontaine 2000, 531). In Israel, this mytho-logical construct comes to be associated with Lilith who tor-mented men in their sleep by robbing them of their semen (Sasson 1979, 78). Such a demon was responsible for wet dreams in a cul-ture where semen/seed was sacred and not to be "wasted." The possibility of a night demon's presence is of interest in that Ruth comes not to torment or steal, but to restore and build. With Ruth, Boaz's seed will produce a child. She is an anti-Lilith.

In this moment of Boaz's vulnerability, Ruth reveals her identity and makes her request. The startled Boaz asks, "Who are you?" She replies, "I am Ruth, your servant; spread your cloak over your servant, for you are next-of-kin" (v. 9). Ruth's answer is both def-erential and inviting. She is Boaz's "handmaid," not the Moabite and not the daughter-in-law of Naomi. In so doing, she chooses Boaz and now offers Boaz the opportunity to reciprocate. Ruth's answer is followed with a request: "Spread your cloak over your servant, for you are next-of-kin." Note that these words are not in keeping with Naomi's script. Naomi told Ruth that after she uncovered Boaz's feet, "he will tell you what to do" (v. 4). Instead, Ruth directs the conversation, making a request of Boaz (Levine 1992, 82). They are both exposed and vulnerable and it evokes the mutual nakedness of Adam and Eve. In Gen 2:25 we read, "And the Man and his wife were both naked, and were not ashamed." The nakedness in the context of Gen 2 (preceding the appearance of the serpent) highlights their vulnerability. So too, the uncover-ing of Boaz and the disclosure of Ruth create a moment of mutual vulnerability. In a male-centered society, Ruth exposes Boaz's feet to make him vulnerable in a way that men universally understand. In so doing, she attempts to even the playing field.

Ruth's vulnerability however, is much greater than that of Boaz. She risks rejection, rape, or molestation with no protection and no recourse. She entrusts her fate to this man. But the act of uncovering his feet before making the request suggests that there is an advantage to Boaz answering positively. If he honors her request, they both will be covered.

Boaz's question to Ruth, "Who are you?" functions on several levels. On a most basic level he wants to know who it is in the darkness that is next to him. In addition to the possible presence of night demons and spirits that intended harm, it is also possible that a woman could take advantage of him in his "contented" state and attempt to force Boaz into an unwanted commitment. Boaz needs to know the identity of the person beside him. On another level, the question evokes a multitude of possibilities around Ruth and her identity. She is a Moabite and a widow. She is daughter-in-law to Naomi. She is an outsider, a gleaner in the field of Boaz who has been called "my daughter" and she is the person who has been defined by her faithfulness. Her identity is shaped by her context. In this almost otherworldly context, the question is rife with possibility, but there is only one possibility that Ruth is interested in. She answers, "I am Ruth, your servant; spread your cloak over your servant, for you are next-of-kin."

Ruth's response offers an identity in a particular context. First of all, it is the first time her name is uttered by a character in the narrative. Ruth finally has a chance to claim an identity and the one she offers has three parts. Of all the possible markers of her identity, she chooses to state her name, followed by two markers that honor her covenant with Naomi. First, "I am Ruth." That she states her name before the identifying markers suggests that Ruth is requesting to be seen as more than just one of Boaz's hand-maidens, but as a specific person and individual within the community who warrants attention. The next part of her disclosure, "your servant," makes use of the term translated as "handmaid." With the appearance of this term we observe a progression in Ruth's conversations with Boaz. Three times Ruth makes reference to herself with Boaz (Nielsen 1997, 73). In their first conversation (2:10), she uses the word "foreigner" to describe herself. Later in response to Boaz's kindness, she refers to herself as a maidservant (3:9). Thus we observe a progression from foreigner to maidservant to handmaid. A handmaid can be of higher status than a maidservant. A woman of high social location can choose to place herself in the role of handmaid. The third part of Ruth's response is an identifier that is relational: "spread your cloak over your servant, for you are next-of-kin." Here the servant is also family and the familial tie requires action on Boaz's part. This is the identity that will allow Ruth to fulfill her vow to Naomi. Moreover, Ruth's disclosure of her identity serves the purpose of identifying Boaz. She is Ruth and he is the redeemer/kinsman. In other words, Boaz is in a position to "buy back" or redeem what was lost to the deceased man, Mahlon. In so doing, he takes on the obligation of preserving the family line. The exchange makes clear that identity in this context is inextricably tied to community.

The location and the time in this chapter form the crux of the narrative. It is the turning point of the novella upon which the resolution of the comedy depends. In this chapter, Boaz and Ruth have an encounter in which the motifs of recognition/nonrecognition are at work. Ruth recognizes or takes note of Boaz on the threshing floor. She uncovers his feet and he subsequently has an encounter that raises the question of identity. Ruth was known to Boaz, but is introduced again, in this new moment, in this particular place, and now he recognizes her, not as Moabite, but as a member of the family. This familial relationship of marriage, unlike that of birth, involved choice. Ruth chose Boaz (3:10) and Boaz in turn will choose Ruth (4:10). There is a marked contrast between the polite speech between Ruth and Boaz in the public space of the field in 2:10-13 and this direct request Ruth makes of him on the threshing floor. Ruth's uncovering of Boaz and her revelation of herself are also reflected in the language of the narrative. Gone is the effusive speech in chapter 2: "May I continue to find favor in your sight, my lord, for you have comforted me and spoken kindly to your servant, even though I am not one of your servants" (2:13). Here the request is clear and simple: "spread your cloak over your servant, for you are next-of-kin (3:9).

Where Ruth's speech is direct, Boaz responds with effusive speech, offering blessing, reassurance, and promise. He blesses her before he answers her: "May you be blessed by the LORD, my daughter; this last instance of your loyalty is better than the first; you have not gone after young men, whether poor or rich" (v. 10). This is in keeping with what we observed of Boaz earlier.

He is quick to praise her and give her special treatment in chapter 2. Moreover, it seems as though Boaz already has plans for Ruth. Her proposal elicits from him more praise for her actions, and then he accepts her offer, with the caveat that there is another relative who has the right of refusal: "though it is true that I am a near kinsman, there is another kinsman more closely related than I" (v. 12). Boaz's response obscures the fact that Ruth is a Moabite and, as such, has no right to have someone redeem or buy back her husband's inheritance on her behalf. Ruth's faithfulness seems to take precedence over everything else.

The mention of the next living male relative is quickly followed by his instructions to "remain this night" (v. 13). Why Boaz asks Ruth to stay the night is not clear. He may be reluctant for her to travel at night or his request may be less selfless in nature.

The setting and circumstances of Ruth's proposal to Boaz evokes Eden. As noted before, they are both vulnerable. Like Eden, they are in a location of abundance and fertility. Her request, however, is one that comes out of a post-Edenic world where women and men are not equal and where they both need covering in the form of clothing, food, and shelter. In order to meet these demands for survival, people create family and work together for the well-being of the unit. If Boaz accepts Ruth's proposal, it means safety for his potential new wife and Naomi, and it provides covering for himself.

The prophet Ezekiel conveys God's account of God's relationship with Israel using the metaphor of marriage. God says, "I spread the edge of my cloak over you, and covered your nakedness: I pledged myself to you and entered into covenant with you...and you became mine" (Ezek 16:8). The word for cloak/robe is "*canaf*" and is the same word used by Boaz in chapter 2 to refer to God's wings. Here, as in Ruth 3, the covering with a cloak is a sign of the marriage covenant.

The act of covering and uncovering in this chapter is noteworthy. Ruth is instructed to put on a cloak (cover herself) and to go down to the threshing floor where she will uncover Boaz and then ask him to cover her with his cloak. The movement from covering to uncovering and uncovering back to covering establishes on a small scale the overall movement of the narrative from abundance/fullness to famine/loss and harvest/redemption.

Evening, the setting of the sun, marks the start of the next day in the Old Testament, and so it is fitting that Ruth's proposal and Boaz's response take place at night, ushering in a "new day." The encounter that will result in a public marriage takes place in relative secret, in the marginal realm of the dark. The pattern in Ruth suggests that God's work, like that of creation itself, begins in darkness.

Boaz instructs Ruth to leave before she can be identified, "it must not be known that the woman came to the threshing floor" (v. 14). Here the concern is for Ruth's reputation (Levine 1992, 82). Boaz sends her home with a gracious gift. He fills her cloak, the one she used to hide her identity, with barley. In so doing, Ruth reverses Naomi's experience in 1:21, "I went away full, but the LORD has brought me back empty." Ruth left empty, but will return to Naomi with a promise and a sign of that promise in the seed that she bears on her back.

Theological Analysis

The encounter between Ruth and Boaz on the threshing floor is a turning point in the narrative. Like the encounter between Ruth and Naomi in chapter 1, it has implications for the remainder of the narrative. In it, the covenant takes the center stage, and for that reason, some attention must be given to the place of the encounter. If the threshing floor is a place commonly associated with the cultic activity of other religions and their fertility worship, there is significant theological meaning in this section. The initial act of redemption for Ruth and Naomi, a Moabite and an Israelite, takes place on the threshing floor. A theological reading of the location suggests that the work of redemption is not limited to a people, a time, or a place. In asking him to redeem her, Ruth the Moabite makes a request of Boaz that will force him to transgress the law. Redemption, as is it portrayed in Ruth, is broad in its scope, suggesting that foreigners (forbidden people) can be redeemed in questionable places. As was the case in chapter 1, the place is marginal and some of the characters, by virtue of their ancestry, are wrong, but the covenant still holds. For a people whose identity is tied to a location, the Ruth narrative reminds its audience that Israel's story extends far beyond the confines of a geographic identity.

In the covenantal language of Exodus, God states God's identity and then issues the terms of the agreement, expectations in light of God's sovereignty. In this passage, Ruth states her identity, but it is in response to Boaz's question, "Who are you?" Moreover, she makes a request of Boaz, "spread your cloak over your servant, for you are next-of-kin." This is a covenant of sorts but in reverse. Ruth's identity is not that of sovereign, but one of servant, and her words are an inquiry and not an imperative. She is placing her hope in Boaz as the one who would be the redeemer.

The reversal of covenant roles also holds in the marriage metaphor. Ruth approaches Boaz directly and offers herself in marriage. With no male relative to offer protection or even to negotiate the terms of marriage, she is without the covering of family. However, Ruth has a family in the person of Naomi and it proves to be sufficient to procuring security. Armed only with the instructions of her mother-in-law, she goes to find the male who will be a covering for herself and Naomi.

A theological reading of these reversals offers several possibilities. At first glance, we are able to observe the extent to which God continues to work wherever and with whomever God chooses. What the threshing floor scene allows for specifically is a deeper exploration of the ways the biblical narrative departs from traditional roles and traditional identity constructs, and their implications.

In the Sinai covenant, God is like the suzerain, who, because of his relationship with Israel (the one who brought them out of bondage/redeemer), lays claim to them and issues the terms of their covenant. God is characterized as being faithful (having *hesed*) and is motivated by a love for this people. Israel is the vassal and is motivated by gratitude and wonder.

Ruth is not the suzerain in the threshing floor scene. Rather, she is the servant who is in the story because of her deep love for

Naomi, evidenced by her covenant to her. Ruth is characterized as being faithful (having *hesed*) and is motivated by a love for Naomi. Ruth lays claim to Boaz and asks him to be their redeemer. Boaz responds with gratitude and wonder.

Who then plays the role of God in the threshing floor narrative? In this reenactment of the covenant in Ruth, the roles of God are divided among the characters across gender and nationality lines. There is no neat division of roles in the chaos of the threshing floor. Rather, Boaz and Ruth share in the godly attributes of faithfulness (*hesed*) and strength (*hayil*).

What this means for a theology of identity is that identity cannot remain limited by gender when it comes into contact with God. The God of Israel is the God of plenty and famine, the God of order and chaos. As such, it is quite possible that the "order" of a given society, roles of people along gender lines, roles for insiders and outsiders, will not survive the encounter with Shaddai. The faithfulness of God, *hesed,* cannot be contained within the people of Israel, and as such, it extends to the people outside of the congregation. Similarly, the faithfulness of God cannot be contained in one gender, male or female. For that reason, the *hesed* in this narrative is found in Ruth and Boaz. Naomi, the barren woman, is Israel who receives redemption and restoration through the cooperation (marriage) of the faithful Ruth and Boaz.

Unlike garments that have the simple function of covering nakedness, the cloak is a protective garment. It is used as an outer layer to shield against the elements, and it can also serve as a bed covering. There is also the reference to the cloak/coat in the Joseph narrative that symbolizes the favor Joseph enjoys. Joseph's robe also serves as an identifying marker. In the Ruth narrative, the garment takes on symbolic meaning. Ruth's request for covering reminds us of her past: she willingly "uncovered" herself when she denied her home and clung to Naomi, and now requests protection from Boaz. The cloak of Boaz represents the safety of a new family. The fact that Boaz is willing to provide this covering is a sign of his favor as well as his faithfulness. Thus the cloak evokes the covenant—it is the covering that God offers to God's people and it is a constant reminder of God's faithfulness and protection. Like the chuppah, or marriage canopy, the cloak symbolized the extent to which the covenant binds God's people to God so that they are now family.

"WHO ARE YOU, MY DAUGHTER?" (3:16-18)

The chapter concludes with Ruth's return home to Naomi who asks her, "How did things go with you, my daughter?" literally, "who are you, my daughter?" Ruth gives Naomi a report of the night's events and Naomi responds with the command, "Wait, my daughter." Naomi told Ruth that Boaz will settle the matter "today."

Literary Analysis

These final verses form a conclusion to the narrative tension. The opening narrative outlines a daring plan, and the closing narrative suggests that the plan was initially successful. There is another kinsman redeemer and although the identity of the redeemer is not clear, redemption for Ruth and Naomi is in the works. Naomi and Boaz do not occupy the same geographic space in the narrative, but they are literarily bound. Both refer to Ruth as daughter and in this chapter, both initiate dialogue with Ruth through the same question. In this chapter, Boaz and Naomi ask Ruth, "Who are you?" Although Naomi's question is often translated, "How did things go with you?" it is, like Boaz's question, asking Ruth to identify herself. To Naomi's question, Ruth's response is an account of what "the man had done for her" (v. 16). In other words, Ruth's identity is one who receives mercy and the hope of redemption. The mercy Ruth receives will include Naomi.

Exegetical Analysis

The Moabite woman does not return empty-handed. Boaz fills her cloak with six measures of barley, which is placed on her back. Now Ruth returns, literally bearing seed that Boaz gave her and with it the promise of new life. The chapter ends as it begins, with a dialogue between Naomi and Ruth about their future. In both sections, Naomi addresses Ruth as *biti,* "my daughter." Naomi begins the exchange with a peculiar question, "Who are you, my daughter?" The question is paradoxical, at best (Davis 2003, 91). The fact that Naomi's question ends with the words "my daughter" mitigates the first part of the question, "who are you?" Most translators interpret Naomi's question to mean that Naomi is inquiring into the well-being of her daughter and not her identity. So we find translations like "How did things go with you, my daughter?" in the NRSV or "How did it go, my daughter?" in the NIV. The KJV preserves the literal sense of the Hebrew, rendering the question, "Who art thou, my daughter?" The literal sense raises a question of its own. If Naomi is asking a literal question, what is she trying to determine?

This is the second time in this chapter that Ruth has been asked "who are you?" and both times it comes from people with whom Ruth has some family connection. Boaz asks this question in verse 9 on the threshing floor and Naomi asks it when she returns from the threshing floor in verse 16. Like the question that is asked of Naomi at 1:19, "Is this Naomi?" this question allows the person being questioned to claim her own identity. When asked this question by Boaz, Ruth identifies herself by name. When asked by her mother-in-law, Ruth answers with the events of the night, concluding by showing the barley accompanied by Boaz's words, "Do not go back to your mother-in-law empty-handed." Boaz's words and the grain make his intentions clear. Naomi understands this and knows the matter will soon be resolved. The anticipation in the literary structure that awaits resolution is mitigated by what we know about the faithfulness of Boaz and Ruth.

The literary lens highlights the fact that this is the third inquiry into Ruth's identity. The repetition of the question highlights the theme of identity. Ruth is an outsider who is noticed as such. Yet each time the question is asked, she is further incorporated into this community. In each question, there is recognition (what is known) and nonrecognition, an acknowledgment that something has changed. Naomi's question assumes that Ruth's public identity could have been transformed as a result of the private encounter with Boaz. In response to Naomi's question, Ruth told Naomi "all that the man had done for her" (v. 16).

This exchange between Ruth and Naomi is the last time either of them speaks in the narrative. Their last words, like their first, are words in dialogue as they negotiate their environment. In chapter 1, Naomi commands her daughters-in-law to "return." In chapter 3, she commands Ruth to "wait." Ruth responds to Naomi's command to return in chapter 1 by insisting on a different kind of return. She will not return to Moab, but she will return with Naomi. After Ruth's vow, Naomi "said no more." Ruth's response to Naomi's instruction to "wait" is met with silence. We can only assume that here Ruth will cooperate fully with Naomi as she set out to do at the beginning of the chapter, saying, "All that you tell me I will do."

Theological Analysis

When Moses returned from his encounter with YHWH on Mount Sinai, he came back with tablets upon which God's words for the people were written—the terms of their covenantal agreement. When Ruth returned from her secret encounter with Boaz, she also brought words: "she told her all that the man had done for her." In addition to the words, she had the barley, which is both provision for the present and seed/a promise for the future. When we observe the dialogue between this part of the Ruth narrative and the giving of the law, we can argue that the law was not intended to be the last word about God's relationship with God's people but the first—a promise of something more that would grow from a planted seed.

Naomi's question, "Who are you, my daughter?" is syntactically awkward, but theologically potent. As it stands in the text, Naomi's question is about identity, which has experienced numerous shifts in the narrative. Does Naomi's question inquire about a change in status? Is it an invitation to name herself? Or does Naomi's question somehow acknowledge the flexibility in identity that is evidenced by Boaz's willingness to redeem her? It is also possible to view this question as analogous with the question raised regarding Naomi in chapter 1. Upon her return from Moab, the women ask, "Is this Naomi?" suggesting a moment of "recognition/nonrecognition." Something has happened to Ruth, and Naomi asks Ruth about her identity to acknowledge some transition. Ruth responds by telling Naomi "all that the man had done for her." Her answer to the question of identity is that she is the recipient of Boaz's faithfulness. The exchange between the women reminds the readers that this story is a story about redemption. As a story of redemption, Ruth asserts that the primary marker of identity for God's people is that they are those who have received and known God's *hesed*/faithfulness.

CHAPTER 4
A DIALOGUE OF IDENTITY

In a comedy, the last act or final chapter is the requisite resolution or happy ending where loose ends are tied, secret identities are revealed, and the tension is resolved. For the story of Ruth, the famine and death in chapter 1 is resolved by the harvest and restoration of family at the end of the book. A tripartite division, which is consistent with the rest of the book, is possible if we divide the chapter based on the content. The fourth chapter has the following components: verses 1-12 detail the exchange that takes place between Boaz and the unnamed next of kin, regarding Ruth and the inheritance of the house of Elimelech; verses 13-17 provide the narrative resolution; and verses 18-22 contain an official genealogy.

Another division of the chapter is possible, based on the observation that 4:1-17 also shifts from the public realm to the private (Sakenfeld 1989, 67). If we divide the chapter this way, verses 1-12 take place at the very public city gate, and verse 13 is set apart as it occupies a private space. This is followed by verses 14-17, which take the reader to the public realm of the women in the village. This division places the marriage of Boaz and Ruth in the center of two public spheres, one occupied by women and the other by men. Spatially, this resembles a number of public gatherings in ancient Near Eastern cultures and contemporary Middle Eastern cultures (including weddings) where it is customary for the women and men to occupy different parts of the room. In a wedding ceremony, bride and groom bridge the chasm. Similarly, in this chapter Boaz and Ruth form a bridge between women and men, and between Israel and Moab.

The division of the chapter according to the realms of public and private suggests that the genealogy in verses 18-22 be considered an epilogue or a later addition. It is in the epilogue that the scope of the story shifts from that of one family to that of the nation Israel. To the role of the genealogy in this narrative we shall return.

"IF YOU WILL REDEEM IT, REDEEM IT" (4:1-12)

Boaz goes to the gate, and the kinsman/redeemer with the right of refusal comes by. Boaz greets him and invites him to sit down with ten elders of the town. Boaz tells the kinsman that there was a piece of land available for redemption through Naomi, widow of their mutual relative Elimelech. The kinsman expresses his interest in purchasing the property. When Boaz mentions that with the property comes a widow, "Ruth the Moabite," the property is no longer of interest to the man. Taking on a childless widow and fathering a child to preserve the deceased relative's name and property rights would infringe upon his own estate. With this refusal, the right of redemption passes to Boaz, and the elders of the community witness a transaction between the two men that makes it official—Boaz will redeem the land *and* Ruth. To confirm the transaction, the kinsman removes his sandal and says the words "Acquire it for yourself" (v. 8). The witnesses at the gate affirm the transaction and offer a blessing upon Ruth.

Literary Analysis

The fourth chapter is the longest of the book and the majority of this chapter focuses on the process of making the bond between Boaz and Ruth legal. It was under the cover of darkness that Ruth and Boaz made their intentions clear. Now, the next day, in the public arena of the gate, the results of the secret meeting are made official.

The first section (vv. 1-12), the transaction of redemption, consists primarily of dialogue. The speakers are Boaz, the kinsman, the elders, and the people at the gate. In addition to these voices there is the important voice of the narrator who provides information on the timing, location, and the transaction of Ruth's redemption. The land that belonged to Elimelech's family would have been used, perhaps claimed in the family's absence. The redeeming of the land entailed buying and regaining control of what had been Elimelech's for Naomi and Ruth's well-being (Farmer 2003, 388). The narrator tells us, "No sooner had Boaz gone up to the gate and sat down there than the next-of-kin, of whom Boaz had spoken, came passing by" (4:1). The text uses the word *hinneh,* a term that conveys an element of surprise or providence, or both. From a literary perspective, this word is a marker of comedic timing, and the reader has the expectation that the identity of Ruth's *levir* will turn out to be Boaz. Both the genre of the story and Naomi's words at the end of chapter 3 assure the reader "the man will not rest, but will settle the matter today" (v. 18).

Boaz's location is at the gate, the place of public transactions and meetings. The redemption of Ruth takes place before observers. Thus, Boaz's right of redemption has layers of witnesses: the people bear witness, the narrator bears witness, and the readers bear witness. Each time the story is told, new audiences bear witness both to the public event and to the "unofficial" moments that lead up to the redemption. The narrator's account of the sandal-exchange ceremony and its explanation is another element that informs the reader that this transaction is legitimate and properly enacted.

Exegetical Analysis

The location and timing of the action in verse 1 is ideal. The final chapter begins at the city gate, the public space where a variety of activities took place. Because it was a high-traffic area, it is here that public transactions requiring witnesses would occur. It is at the gate that Boaz would likely encounter or determine the whereabouts of his relative and it is at the gate that Boaz would find the elders of the city, people who could serve as witnesses. Boaz's arrival at the gate coincides with the appearance of the relative who has the right to redeem. The text uses the term *hinneh,* often translated as "behold" or "lo" or "here." This type of coincidental meeting has happened before. In chapter 2, Boaz the landowner just happens to come to the field where Ruth is gleaning. Again, the word *"hinneh"* is used to convey the unexpected nature of a character's appearance.

In a comedy, this timing is expected because in a comedy the story turns on unexpected meetings, twists in plot involving location and mistaken identity. In this narrative, the plot is advanced by the juxtaposition of encounters and locations. Here, Boaz encounters the relative he wants to see at the time and place he desires. This meeting brings to mind the encounter between Ruth and Naomi in an undisclosed, in-between space in chapter 1, that between Boaz and Ruth in broad daylight in the fields (chapter 2), and Ruth's and Naomi's planned meeting between Ruth and Boaz in the dark on the threshing floor (chapter 3). Each of these encounters led to a decision or choice that was a turning point in the story. Cumulatively, the encounters in chapter 3 contributed to those in the final chapter. In this final meeting the expectation is that the problem of security and proper identity for Ruth will be resolved. Either Boaz or the kinsman will redeem Ruth. The fact that he shows up at just the right time is a good sign.

In a story where names, such as Naomi/Mara, Mahlon, Chilion, Ruth, Orpha, and Elimelech, have played such a central role, it is quite noticable tthat the name of this relative is not revealed. Boaz calls to his kinsman, "Come over, friend; sit down here." The NRSV provides the word "friend" for the Hebrew *peloni almoni,* meaning "so-and-so" or "such-and-such." A "so-and-so" is a "what's his name," someone who will not have a major role in in this narrative. Like the names Mahlon and Chilion, the name *"peloni almoni"* rhymes, lending a singsong, almost mocking tone to the name of the relative (Campbell 1975,

74). Mahlon and Chilion, as their names suggest, are lacking in strength (*hayil*), and the potential redeemer, by virtue of his actions, is lacking in faithfulness (*hesed*). Ruth is a woman of strength (*hayil*) and faithfulness (*hesed*), qualities this would-be husband is lacking. Only a Boaz, a man of strength and faithfulness, will do.

The action in verses 1-12 mirror the scene with Naomi, Ruth, and Orpah in chapter 1. In the first chapter, Naomi tries to send Ruth away and in the fourth chapter, Boaz wants to acquire Ruth. In both scenes, a third party is involved. Orpah (back of neck) is named and the would-be redeemer is not, but in both narrative segments, the third party disappears from the story so that Ruth can be bound (to Naomi in chapter 1 and Boaz in this concluding chapter).

In verses 2-5, Boaz dominates the action and the conversation. In many ways he orchestrates the events here, commanding first the would-be redeemer and then the elders to sit down, just as Naomi orchestrates the events that took place in chapter 3. Moreover, Boaz's command issued first to his relative and then the elders to "sit" echoes the instruction Naomi gave to Ruth at the end of the previous chapter when she returned from her night on the threshing floor. The assembly, or sitting of these men, reminds the reader of Ruth in another location with her mother-in-law, awaiting her fate.

Once the right people are in place, Boaz states his business: there is land for sale from Naomi the widow of Elimelech and the relative is first in line to buy, followed by Boaz. Boaz's presentation comes as a surprise to the reader. Here we thought the business at hand was a husband for Ruth. Boaz's mention of the land that must be redeemed reminds us of the larger issues of family, inheritance, and name. Naomi cannot own or inherit this land. In order to preserve an attachment to the land she must do so through marriage. Here Ruth is the key to achieving this goal. When Boaz speaks to the relative about buying the land, he speaks on Naomi's behalf. Boaz's speech is polite and elaborate, like his words to Ruth in chapter 2. A rough translation of Boaz's opening words to his relative in 4:4 are as follows, "And I, I said,

111

I will uncover your ears, saying." A cursory glance suggests there are more words in this construction than necessary. Perhaps Boaz wants to draw attention to what is about to transpire. It could simply be another example of Boaz's effusive public speech, which we have witnessed in chapters 2 and 3. The image of uncovering the ears, however, reminds the reader of the literal and figurative uncovering and covering that took place on the threshing floor on the previous night. Moreover, this uncovering of the ears reminds the reader of the differences between hearing and understanding. Boaz understands the situation that he is telling his relative about and he will give the information in a way that will lead to the outcome Boaz desires.

When offered the option to buy, the relative responds, "I will redeem it" (v. 4). It is only after the relative offers to redeem the land that Boaz adds a piece of pertinent information, namely that the land comes with a Moabite widow and the dead man's name must be maintained. The way in which the information is disclosed places Boaz in league with his ancestress Tamar in Gen 38. Tamar, in her plan to secure her right to a son, has information that Judah does not. She knows that Judah is on his way to Timnah, and like Boaz, she positions herself by the gate to create an encounter. In the exchange between Boaz and his relative, like that between Judah and Tamar, the person who desires the exchange carefully discloses information to manipulate another. Tamar allows Judah to think she is a prostitute and Boaz chooses to describe Ruth as "the Moabite, the widow of the dead man" (v. 5). Boaz's language to describe Ruth bears little resemblance to his description of her the night before. Here she is a Moabite, a "wife of the dead." This casts Ruth as an obligation and a foreigner, hardly the faithful woman he described the night before as faithful and worthy (3:10-11). Boaz carefully dispenses information to the kinsman, and he is successful. The relative has a change of heart in verse 6. The redemption of the land would require the lessening of his own estate if he is to maintain the line of Elimelech and Mahlon. His sentiments sound similiar to those of Onan, the would-be *levir* of Tamar, who does not want to lessen his own inheritance by redeeming the inheritance of another.

If we follow the argument that the actions of Ruth and Naomi in chapter 3 revisit and redeem the story of Lot's daughters in Gen 19, then it is also quite possible that Boaz's redemption of Ruth in chapter 4 creates a dialogue with the story of Judah and Tamar in Gen 38 that is redemptive for Judah. Here Boaz willingly takes on the role of *levir* when the kinsman expresses concern over his own inheritance. In the role of Judah, Boaz does knowingly what Judah did unknowingly: he ensures the continuation of the line by taking on the responsibility abandoned by another.

The public rite of transfer takes place in verses 7-10. Here, the unnamed kinsman takes off his sandal and gives it to Boaz, symbolizing the transfer of the right to purchase. Then Boaz states before the witnesses that he takes possession of all that belonged to Elimelech and his family, including Ruth, the widow of Mahlon, "in order that the name of the dead may not be cut off from his kindred" (v. 10). The word for sandal in this passage is "*na'al.*" An obsolete form of this word may have meant "levirate wife" (Brown, Driver, and Briggs 2001, 653).

The sandal ceremony is introduced: "Now this was the custom in former times in Israel concerning redeeming and exchanging: to confirm a transaction, one party took off a sandal and gave it to the other; this was the manner of attesting in Israel" (v. 7). This introduction places the practice in the past relative to the audience. On a literary level, the narrator is explaining the behavior of the characters so that the audience can understand. On a historical level, it raises questions around the composition or dating of Ruth. This is a potential clue to the time of writing if the narrator has to explain older practices to an audience. The value of this clue, however, is mitigated by the history of oral transmission. It is possible that the story of Ruth existed as a folktale long before it was carefully crafted into the romantic novella that we have in the Bible. If that is the case, the explanation about the sandal ceremony could have come into the story at a later stage, for a later audience.

It is also possible that the explanation makes a distinction between what happens in this chapter and the situation described in Deuteronomy 25:5-11. When a man refuses to perform the duty of *levir,* the widow goes to the elders at the gate and tells them her brother-in-law is not willing to serve as *levir* (Deut 25:7). The elders will call the brother and speak to him. If he still refuses, the widow was to go to him in the presence of those assembled, remove his sandal, spit in his face, and say, "This is what is done to the man who does not build up his brother's house" (v. 9). This man's family will be known as the "house of him whose sandal was pulled off" (v. 10).

The sandal ceremony also serves another function. In chapters 3 and 4, garments are in the service of the narrative. In chapter 3, Ruth covers herself and later reveals or "makes herself known" to the man. This revelation involves uncovering Boaz and then asking him for protection or covering. In chapter 4, the next-of-kin who refuses the role of redeemer removes a garment, here a sandal, and hands it over to Boaz. This act represents the "conveying of goods or rights from one party to another" (Berlin 1989, 414).

The removal of the sandal in Deut 25 is clearly a mark of shame and dishonor and it is not clear that the ritual in Ruth is intended to convey shame. Nevertheless, the removal of the sandal is connected with the man who will not be the redeemer. The transfer of garment evokes another element of the Judah and Tamar story in Gen 38. In that narrative, there is covering and uncovering, but there is also the transfer of personal items. When Judah mistakes Tamar for a prostitute, he gives her his signet and his cord as a sign of his pledge. It is possible that the sandal functions as an identifying marker as well. It is the signet and cord that Tamar produces in order to save or "redeem" herself when Judah orders that she be stoned. Finally, the next-of-kin's removal of his sandal exposes his feet and evokes the previous chapter where Ruth uncovered Boaz's feet.

Boaz calls to the elders to bear witness to the kinsman, who says "redeem for yourself," which they do. The sandal ceremony invites the readers to stand as witness to the transaction that makes him the rightful redeemer. In verses 4-12, there are numerous references to "witness" and "name." Those assembled by Boaz bear witness to a transfer of property (vv. 4, 9, 10, 11) that preserves a name (vv. 5 and 10). The name is preserved through offspring who carry the name, so that it is repeated, remembered, and not forgotten, or cut off from the land. Interestingly, the relative's unwillingness to be the redeemer results in the omission of his name in this narrative.

The witnesses then offer a blessing that includes the names of ancestors: "May the LORD make the woman who is coming into your house like Rachel and Leah, who together built up the house of Israel. May you produce children in Ephrathah and bestow a name in Bethlehem; And, through the children that the LORD will give you by this young woman, may your house be like the house of Perez, whom Tamar bore to Judah" (vv. 11b-12). In a narrative where names have played such a prominent role, the reader is immediately drawn to the names invoked in the blessing. First the elders evoke the names of Rachel and Leah, wives of Jacob, mothers of the tribes of Israel. This is a typical blessing in that it calls to remembrance the ancestral roots and invokes the history of fertility with the hope of bringing it into the present. What is of interest, however, is the fact that Rachel, the younger, mother of four (two from Rachel and two from her handmaid, Bilhah) comes before Leah, the first wife and mother of nine (one daughter and six sons of her own, and two from her handmaid Zilpah in Gen 29:31–30:21). The mention of Rachel first contains a number of possibilities. One is the possibility that Boaz is already married, as Jacob was when he married Rachel. The mention of Rachel first also carries the possibility that this levirate union may be more than one of duty—Boaz may actually love Ruth just as Jacob loved Rachel. Finally, listing the younger daughter and second wife first implies a reversal of sorts, and clearly the marriage of a Moabite widow to a prominent man in the house of Judah is a reversal. The outsider, the "foreign woman," is welcomed with a blessing of the wives of Jacob.

The second matriarch mentioned in this blessing is Tamar, who has already been discussed. Tamar's mention in the blessing strengthens the structural and other literary connections to her story. In Tamar's story, we observe the themes of levirate marriage and the use of mistaken identity (often facilitated by garments) to continue the family line. In Ruth, the theme of identity takes its shape along the lines of insiders and outsiders. Whereas the Tamar story turns on a case of mistaken identity, the characters in the narrative are clear on Ruth's identity as an outsider. Ruth's actions demonstrate that those identifying markers do not restrict her function in the narrative. Ruth's actions force a new understanding of identity, in the same way that Tamar's actions force a change in Judah. Both of these women also produce sons who allow the family to continue.

Theological Analysis

The literary lens sheds light on the timing and location of this final "act" in the comedy. It informs us that in a comedy, timing is everything. It is the difference between resolution and chaos. So too, the theological lens exposes an additional layer of meaning. The term "*hinneh*," used to indicate the unexpected nature of the meeting between Boaz and his relative, could also be used to indicate that the meeting was not so unexpected. *Hinneh* often takes on a theological dimension, at times referring to a revelation from God or a response to God. In the Ruth narrative, this term serves double duty, simultaneously conveying surprise and implying the presence of God in the narrative. If that is the case, the narrative tells a story about chance happenings that when read theologically, informs the reader that nothing is left to chance. In a story that lacks direct references to God's action in human affairs, the timing of Boaz's encounters with Ruth in chapters 2 and 3, and his encounter with the kinsman in chapter 4, connote some level of divine sanction.

Redemption, the practice of buying back that which was lost, has connotations that are inescapably theological. Israel uses the metaphor of family to describe her covenant relationship with God, and redemption is something one relative does for another in order to restore and maintain the family. In many senses, this is what the story is all about—the salvation of Elimelech's line. Whit this lens, Boaz is readily cast in the role of God, the redeemer.

Although redemption is a common theme in Scripture, the way

redemption takes place in Ruth is most uncommon. Behind the traditional sandal exchange ceremony is the nighttime encounter on the threshing floor and the gleaning in Boaz's fields at Naomi's suggestion and the pledge of fidelity Ruth made to Naomi. The traditional exchange and ritual of redemption in chapter 4 is supported by untraditional or countertraditional events, which for the most part have been associated with the Moabite Ruth. It is this Moabite who is named, however, and the next-of-kin who is not. A theological lens will reveal a testament to God's work of redemption. Ruth recasts our traditional understanding of redemption by uncovering the countertraditions that constitute God's work in the world. As a result, redemption in this survival story is not limited to just a few.

The blessing, a sign of God's favor in Scripture, is another example of a traditional practice that contains countertraditional elements. In the ancestral narratives we observe the following examples. When God calls Abraham in Gen 12:2, God promises "I will bless you, and make your name great, so that you will be a blessing." Abraham's daughter-in-law, Rebekah, receives a blessing from her family as she prepares to leave home and marry Isaac: "May you, our sister, become thousands of myriads; may your offspring gain possession of the gates of their foes" (Gen 24:60). Jacob receives a blessing from his father, Isaac, as he prepares to leave home in Gen 28:3: "May El Shaddai bless you and make you fruitful and numerous, that you may become a company of peoples. May he give to you the blessing of Abraham, to you and to your offspring with you, so that you may take possession of the land where you now live as an alien—land that God gave to Abraham."

In these narratives, the blessings are associated with progeny. The original promise God made to Abraham in Gen 12 requires him to leave his home so that God can make of him a great nation. This promise was threefold. God promised descendants, land, and blessing. In Gen 24, Rebekah is leaving home to marry Isaac. In Gen 28, Jacob is returning to the land of his mother, Rebekah, to find a bride among his relatives. The blessings in the patriarchal narratives express a desire on the part of the witnesses that the newly married or about to be married would fulfill the blessing of Abraham.

As a result of agreeing to take Ruth as his wife, Boaz will receive a threefold blessing as well. He procures land when he marries Ruth, he will have descendants as a result of his marriage to Ruth, and he receives and is a blessing. That the blessing given to Boaz hearkens back to the patriarchal period suggests a return to the building up of Israel. This reference provides an interesting connection to both of Ruth's possible dates. If Ruth was written around the time of the Davidic monarchy, then David's Israel is seen as a rebuilding of the nation after the chaos of the period of the judges and the uncertainty during the time of Saul. If Ruth was written during the time of the return, it speaks to the building up of the nation that suggests that God will rebuild out of the chaos of exile. If Boaz's redemption of Elimelech's house is symbolic of the rebuilding of Israel after exile, we come to a different vision of the restored nation than that presented in Ezra and Nehemiah. This image of Israel includes those outsiders who make YHWH their God.

This understanding of the patriarchal blessing is in tension with the personal blessing that Jacob wrests from Esau through deception in Gen 27. The personal blessing of Isaac is for one child and cannot be used again. The patriarchal blessing is one blessing that is passed from generation to generation, affirming God's promise to Abraham. The blessing is addressed to Boaz but concerns Ruth. Here, she is not Ruth but "the woman who is coming into your house" (v. 11). She is compared to Rachel, Leah, and Tamar. With the invocation of the matriarchs, Ruth is not just *biti,* or "daughter," to Naomi and Boaz (chapter 2), she is daughter to the matriarchs. Like Tamar, Ruth is remembered in the tradition of Scripture and is remembered in a positive light.

That Rachel and Leah are mentioned is to be expected in a blessing about fertility since they are the mothers of the twelve tribes of Israel. Actually, the Genesis narrative clearly states that there were four women who gave birth to the twelve sons of Jacob. Rachel and Leah were aided by their maid surrogates, Zilpah and Bilhah (Gen 30:4-13). What are we to make of the fact that they are not mentioned? Is Ruth being likened to the matriarchs Leah and Rachel, or will she be subsumed in history like Zilpah and Bilhah? Perhaps the answer comes with the mention of the third woman, Tamar. Tamar, like Ruth, goes to some lengths to preserve the line. Both stories involve levirate marriage, both raise the question of identity, and both involve a sexual encounter that is planned by the woman. Perhaps the blessing is identifying Ruth as someone who has broken through the barriers of the cultural norms, like Perez (Tamar's son), who broke through to claim the birthright. Here that act is blessed by the elders of the community, and Ruth, the woman coming into the house of Boaz, is blessed as well.

"So Boaz took Ruth" (4:13-17)

Boaz marries Ruth and she has a son. The women of the community offer a blessing. Naomi becomes the nurse of the child, who is named Obed. Obed's son was Jesse and Jesse's son was David.

Literary Analysis

The central moment of this chapter is unlike the others in terms of its size and its shape. Although the account of Boaz's and Ruth's marriage is surrounded by dialogue, it contains none of its own. Ruth and Boaz come together in marriage and have a son. The future of Naomi and Ruth is secured. The names of Elimelech and Mahlon are preserved. The characters and the readers will encounter a narrative resolution and a historical unit that creates a new understanding of identity—one that not only includes an outsider but acknowledges her role in the community's redemption.

Verse 13 contains the elements of marriage that are "standard" in Hebrew narrative, namely, a man takes a woman as his wife and she conceives. The marriage of Ruth and Boaz is not only the redemption of Ruth; it is the redemption of the plot. In a few words, the tragedies and uncertainties of chapter 1 are resolved.

The famine is over and God has provided for God's people. Ruth's marriage to Boaz and the child that results from their union ensures that the line of Elimelech will not be forgotten. Moreover, there is security for the widows.

In this central moment/movement, the location has shifted from the public realm to that of the private and back again. The official redemption in the gate leads to a marriage, and what takes place in the privacy of the marriage chamber has implications that reach outward to the extended family of Naomi and beyond. This action also serves to transition us from one public location to another. The birth of a son in verse 13 shifts us from the men at the city gate in verses 1-12 to an assembly of women in verses 14-17.

The women of the community speak on the occasion of the birth of the child named Obed. Their words take the form of a blessing, first of the Lord, followed by words about Obed and his mother, Ruth. True to the comedic style, the final part of the narrative is brief. The happy ending has been achieved and a blessing/benediction has been offered. The blessing offered by the women creates a dialogue with several other passages within the Ruth narrative. The women's blessing serves as a counterpart to the blessing offered by the men earlier in the chapter. The men's blessing (4:11-12) precedes the marriage and expresses the hope that God will bless Ruth with children so that Boaz will have a *"name* in Bethlehem," and a *"house* ... like the house of Perez." These references to name and house speak to the elements central to identity in this context. The blessing is for a firm establishment of Boaz and his descendants, evoking the sense of *hayil* or strength. The women's blessing comes on the other side of Obed's birth. "Blessed be the LORD, who has not left you this day without next-of-kin" (v. 14). Here the blessing speaks of God's faithfulness or *hesed*. This second blessing also refers to the establishment of a name, "and may his *name* be renowned in Israel!" Whose name is being referred to in this blessing: Boaz or Obed? Since they are a part of the same family line, it applies to both. The identity of the redeemer seems to extend beyond one person, as does the identity of Obed's mother. Ruth gives birth and Naomi is the child's nurse.

Here the story seems to reflect a more expansive or inclusive understanding of identity.

The women's blessing also serves as a response to Naomi's words about her forlorn state at the end of chapter 1. Upon her return to Bethlehem, Naomi laments that Shaddai has brought her back "empty" and "brought calamity upon [her]" (1:21). In the final chapter, God has proven to be faithful as the one who provides a *"restorer* of life and a *nourisher* of your old age" (v. 15).

Exegetical Analysis

In verse 13, Boaz "took" Ruth as his wife. The standard terminology for marriage, "take a wife," is used here. The taking of a wife entails consummation that "enacts" the marriage. It is also central to the building up of a family, maintaining the line, and preserving one's name on the earth. Thus, the first part of the verse is formulaic and as a result is assuring. Things are as they should be. The marriage provides security for the women and builds up the family with the birth of children, preserving the name of the deceased. Boaz's taking of a wife is in contrast to Mahlon and Chilion's taking of their Moabite wives in 1:4. Here the rarely used verb "to lift up" describes the action. Ultimately, the standard term for marriage here in chapter 4 introduces the possibility that the marriage of Boaz and Ruth is somehow more legitimate than the marriage of Mahlon and Ruth. Once again the Moabitess is taken as a wife, but this time, the verb suggests this is a "proper" union.

It should be noted that in one midrash (a collection of Jewish commentary on Scripture), Boaz is clearly older, eighty, and he dies on the day of the wedding. This leaves Ruth as a widow once again, but not as one bereft, as Naomi is described in 1:5. This time, there is a son whose very presence means the work of redemption has been realized. This midrash reflects a perspective that is not so concerned about the relationship between Ruth and Boaz as it is one about their role in the preservation of the line.

In verses 14-17, the women offer a blessing for Naomi, which first blesses YHWH, the provider of the redeemer. Like the blessing that the men give Boaz, the names of Ruth and Boaz are not mentioned. Boaz's blessing mentions "the woman who is coming into your house" (v. 11) and Naomi's mentions her "next-of-kin" and her "daughter-in-law" (vv. 14, 15). The only names in this section are those of YHWH and the baby, who is given the name "Obed" by the "women of the neighborhood" (v. 17). The lack of names in the blessing leaves open for question the identity of the "next-of-kin" or redeemer. Is the redeemer here Boaz or Obed? Or is it possibly YHWH? The identity of the redeemer depends upon the context within which the blessing is read. Verse 14 suggests that the redeemer is Boaz, in part because he was introduced as a potential redeemer in 2:1, and in the preceding narrative in chapter 4, he has just redeemed the property of his deceased relative, acquired his widow, and had a son. Ruth 4:15 continues to praise the redeemer with a phrase that introduces the real possibility of another identity for the redeemer: "He shall be to you a restorer of life and a nourisher of your old age; for your daughter-in-law who loves you, who is more to you than seven sons, has borne him."

Verse 15 suggests the next-of-kin is the child born to Boaz and Ruth, the "placeholder" for Mahlon. The phrase "restorer of life" is literally "returner of life" based on the word "*sub*," which is the word used to describe the return of Naomi and Ruth to Bethlehem, and it is the word invoked by Naomi to describe her state—that YHWH "brought her back" empty. Here the recurrence of the term "*sub*" offers still another possibility for the identity of the redeemer and that is YHWH. YHWH brought bread to Bethlehem and brought the widows to Bethlehem. YHWH opened Ruth's womb and allowed her to conceive.

The identity confusion in the blessing spills over into the following two verses where the women name the child. Usually it is the mother or father who names the child. Obed means "servant," perhaps acknowledging that his existence serves the purpose of upholding a deceased ancestor's name and place. By virtue of being born, Obed preserves the future. Not only do the women name the child, but Naomi takes the child and "laid him in her bosom, and became his nurse" (v. 16). Again, this action leads to confusion of role and identity. First, what does this mean? Does Naomi literally nurse the child? Second, where is Ruth in all of this? Does she matter only in her ability to bear a child? I will offer a few observations.

First, the words used to describe the transfer consist of two phrases. The first set of words, "laid him in her bosom," appear elsewhere in the Bible. The "bosom" is a part of male and female anatomy. Sarai gave Hagar to Abram as a wife into his "bosom" (KJV), connoting "embrace" or closeness in Gen 16:5. Moses placed his hand in his bosom at God's command in Exod 4:6-8. Thus, Ruth's act of placing the child on Naomi's bosom may simply connote that Naomi held the child. The second phrase, "and [she] became his nurse" has as its root the word "'aman," which connotes support, caregiving, nourishing, or childrearing. Like the word for bosom, it is an act performed by women and men. In Esth 2:20 it is used to describe Mordecai's care of Esther. This word is also used to connote faithfulness and fidelity, which reminds us of the faithfulness/hesed we associate with Ruth.

The debate among biblical interpreters tends to focus on whether the transfer of the child is symbolic or literal. What we know for sure is that Naomi is not forgotten when the child is born. Obed's birth results in restoration for Naomi and validation for Ruth. The "transfer" of Obed to Naomi, whether symbolic or more substantive, means that Obed has an Israelite "mother." In this chapter there is a marriage followed by an "adoption," the two practices used as metaphors that speak to God's relationship with God's people. The identity confusion could be seen as a spilling over of blessing. God's blessings by their very nature are larger than the people who receive them.

Second, the reference to nursing takes us to Naomi's mention of El-Shaddai in chapter 1. The comedic element of reversals is present in this section of the story. In 1:19-22, Naomi returns to Bethlehem and the women of the town ask, "Is this Naomi?" This is a question of identity, to which Naomi asserts another identity. "Call me Mara," she insists, because "Shaddai has dealt bitterly with me." In chapter 4, however, the women do not ask a question about Naomi's identity. Rather, they make an assertion about YHWH. In the earlier narrative, Naomi justifies her name change based on Shaddai's dealing with her. He has dealt "harshly" with her. Naomi has gone from full to empty. YHWH has "afflicted" her and Shaddai has brought "evil" upon her. In chapter 4, the women affirm YHWH's goodness by acknowledging what God has done as a "restorer of life" and "nourisher of your old age" (v. 15). The praise of God as redeemer does not overshadow the acknowledgment of Ruth's faithfulness. This designation of Ruth as better than seven sons is most high praise. Whether the placement of the child in Naomi's bosom is symbolic or literal, it serves the narrative function of undoing the emptiness in chapter 1. El Shaddai, "God of the breast," withholds nourishment in chapter 1. In chapter 4, Naomi's restoration and blessing are demonstrated in her "nursing" of the baby Obed. Naomi is restored and the famine, emptiness, and barrenness from the first chapter has not only been resolved, but reversed.

Third, I have described Ruth's words to Naomi in chapter 1 as performative speech; in other words, Ruth's vow does not simply describe an intention to stay with her mother-in-law. The words enact a reality in the same way that the words spoken in a marriage ceremony, "I take thee...," do. Because this passage in chapter 4 is in dialogue with the scene in chapter 1, it is quite likely that the words of the women here are operating in the same sense. The women decree and acknowledge the end of Naomi's woes and they make Ruth's and Obed's roles in the family official. Their decree is parallel to Boaz's marriage of Ruth in this chapter.

Fourth, the description of Obed's birth and the subsequent blessing raises a question about genre, namely, is this story an extended birth narrative in addition to being a comedy? We have observed birth narratives to have the following characteristics:

- extenuating circumstances surround the birth of the child, most often involving the mother's barrenness and/or age;
- the resulting birth is clearly miraculous;
- the naming of the child is significant and sometimes unusual; and
- a birth narrative is used to introduce a character who will play a central role in the ensuing narrative.

If Ruth is read as a birth narrative, Naomi and Ruth are both candidates for the role of mother in that they both face barriers to childbirth. Both are widows. Naomi is older, and it is possible that her age prohibits her from conceiving. Ruth is a Moabite who is to be shunned by Israel. Moreover, she has been married for approximately ten years and is childless. As is the case in most birth narratives, Obed's birth is connected to the work of God. Ruth 4:13 specifically states, "When they came together, the LORD made her conceive."

The naming of the child is both significant and unusual. If Ruth is a birth narrative, which character is being introduced as key to the ensuing narrative? This is not immediately clear. Naomi is a major character in the narrative, as is Ruth, after whom the book is named. Moreover, the genealogy directs the attention of the reader to David, the grandson of Obed.

Although the genre markers for a birth narrative exist in the book of Ruth, the characters do not easily fit into the prescribed roles. The role of the barren mother would be shared by Naomi and Ruth and the role of the anticipated child should be Obed but could also be David. If read this way, all the characters—Ruth, Naomi, and Boaz—are secondary to the role of the children. This reading places all three characters in supporting roles to Obed and David.

The lack of clarity around prescribed roles and the presence of the genealogy raise the question about the narrative function of this piece as a birth narrative. In other words, if Ruth is a birth narrative, whose birth is it describing? Here I offer a suggestion.

One possibility is that the story of Ruth is a symbolic birth narrative analogous with that of Samuel. First Sam 1 has the story of Samuel's birth in 1 Sam 1 has the elements of a birth narrative, but the etymology of the child's name is problematic. Samuel means "his name is God," not "I have *asked* him of the LORD" (emphasis added), as Hannah states in 1 Sam 1:20. The verb "to ask" is *sa'al,* which is the basis for the name Saul, the first king of Israel. This "confusion" around the names and their meanings led Robert Polzin to argue that the first chapter of Samuel was a birth narrative for Samuel that had an allegorical function as a birth narrative for the monarchy. This possibility that the birth narrative is detailing two births is further supported by the frequent occurrences of the verb *sa'al* in the chapter. (Polzin, 1989, 26)

To what extent does the "confusion" around the roles in Ruth open up the possibility that Ruth is a birth narrative that has more than one function? I suggest that Ruth could be read as a birth narrative for Obed, David, and the nation Israel after the return. Ruth then is a birth narrative that includes an adoption. There are two ways to become part of a family. One is by birth and the other is by choice (marriage or adoption). Seen in this light, Israel is reminded it was not always God's people. The people were "other/outsider" and God chose them. Bringing the outsider in is core to Israel's identity. In the postexilic setting of Ezra–Nehemiah, where the sending away of foreign wives and children is a sign of loyalty to Israel and YHWH, Ruth offers an alternative vision. Bringing the outsider into the family is the basis of Israel's origins and identity. In other words, Ruth and Naomi represent Israel and her foreign wives and children who are able to come back. The foreign wives accept YHWH, are married legitimately, and the children are adopted.

Theological Analysis

The verse that bears witness to Boaz and Ruth's marriage includes the phrase "the LORD made her conceive" (v. 13). In the midst of all the concerns in chapter 1 about the public and private realm, the proper transaction of business, and the all-important redemption of the line are five words that remind the reader that the actions of the characters in the story are supported and guided by YHWH. The LORD is the giver of life, the one who opens and closes wombs. YHWH gives his people bread (1:6) and it is YHWH's consideration of Ruth that allows for the line to continue. For an exilic or postexilic audience, the idea of God bringing people home and then blessing the people with fertility is a hopeful message that affirms their identity as God's people. God will return and restore. These are manifestations of God's work of building up "the house of Israel." What is of theological interest here is the fact that God's act of redemption and restoration includes those who have long been outside the people of Israel. In this image of the house of Israel, some of the mortar and brick comes from Moab. Since Moab comes from Lot, nephew of Abraham, the narrative can be seen as reincorporating those who walked away, as Lot did from Abraham (Gen 13).

The blessing of the women in verses 14-17 comes into the narrative without an introduction and takes center stage. As indicated in the earlier section, the words make it official that Naomi's calamities have been reversed. From a theological perspective, the words of the women bear witness to a God who is at work through a variety of circumstances. That God is associated with Naomi's emptiness in chapter 1 and her fullness in chapter 4 speaks to the ever-present faithfulness of God. God is present in the famine, death, and barrenness. God is present in the harvest and new life. In spite of the circumstances or the timing or the season, God is faithful.

"NOW THESE ARE THE DESCENDANTS..." (4:18-22)

The final four verses of the Ruth story are a brief genealogy. It begins with Perez and ends with David, the beloved king of Israel.

Literary Analysis

The genealogy is a genre that is distinct from the rest of the narrative and extends beyond the scope of the story. For this reason, many scholars believe it to be a later addition. Like the temporal references with which the story begins, the genealogy reaches back before "the days that the judges ruled" with the mention of Perez, son of Tamar and Judah. Concluding with the mention of David, the genealogy goes beyond the time of Ruth and Boaz, allowing the reader to see how the actions in this narrative are pivotal in the salvation history of Israel. The placement of the genealogy in these final four verses focuses our attention on its specific function or purpose the specific purpose in the story.

The genealogy stands in the position of the coda, the concluding passage. In comedic terms, the genealogy is in the position of the epilogue. The coda and the epilogue serve the same purposes: to mark the conclusion of the story, to form a bridge between the world of the story and that of the audience, and to tie a lesser known story into a known history. A narrative that includes a coda can have more than one ending. One is for the narrative action and one connects the completed story to another context, be it that of the audience or that of another story. In the story of Ruth, the first ending in 4:17 completes the action of the narrative. The second ending combines one story line with another. Now the story of David has its origins in the story of Ruth in much the same way that many begin the story of the civil rights movement in the United States with the story of Rosa Parks, who refused to give up her bus seat.

Exegetical Analysis

Genealogies are the parts of the text most modern readers tend to ignore. They list names that are unrecognizable and hard to pronounce, and most readers are hard-pressed to see the connection between the genealogy and the narrative. Scholars differ in their understanding of the role of genealogies in the Bible. Many look to these family lists as historical records. As such their value is tied to their historical accuracy. Unfortunately, many genealogies in the Bible are selective and unapologetically subjective; they do not always appear to be concerned with historical accuracy in the way that later biblical scholars are. That is not to say that genealogies have no historical value or that oral traditions are incapable of maintaining accurate records. To the contrary, the depth and level of accuracy in oral traditions has been acknowledged. What anthropological studies reveal about oral traditions is that they are fluid, but not because the keepers of the tradition had poor recall. Rather, fluidity allows for the tradition to be shaped to meet the need of the story. Although the storyteller may know the names of the ancestors for thirty generations or more, she may only need to name the last ten for the purpose of a particular story. Later treatments of genealogies rightly suggest that genealogies have roles that are other than historical—that they may also serve political and social purposes (Wilson 1977, 54). These studies of genealogies reveal different genealogical formats concluding that different forms may have had different functions.

The genealogy in Ruth can operate in a variety of ways. It can be historical, it can be political and social, and it can have a theological function or purpose. The genealogy in verses 18-22 is an expansion of verse 17. The narrative of verse 17 is in many ways a fitting conclusion to the story. A son is born to Ruth and in verse 17 the "women of the neighborhood," who appeared at the end of chapter 1, name the child saying, "A son has been born to Naomi." The child is named Obed, which is a participle form of the verb 'abad, meaning server or worshiper. The verse concludes with a brief genealogy: "he [Obed] became the father of Jesse, the father of David." That the story of this family leads to David is already a part of the narrative. What then do the verses in 18-22 add? The fuller genealogy with ten generations is an "official" version of what precedes in the narrative. Moreover, this longer version allows for a genealogy that places Boaz and David in places of honor, the seventh and tenth positions (Sakenfeld, 1989, 85).

The historical connection between Ruth and David is not one that needs to be proved so much as defended. Ruth, formerly known as "Ruth the Moabite," is in the family line of David. The pressing concerns are around the political, social, and literary implications of such a genealogy, which are dependent on the dating and placement of Ruth in the canon. If Ruth was written during the reign of David, then Ruth's hesed and other virtues make David's place as king legitimate in spite of his Moabite blood. If Ruth was written during the time of Ezra–Nehemiah, then the genealogy challenges the legitimacy of racial purity that is in Ezra–Nehemiah.

Perhaps the goal of the genealogy is not to tear down the notion of racial purity so much as it is to remind the audience that all identities are constructed. As such, they are constantly open to new constructions, new orderings. In the Old Testament the one element that is not negotiable is the centrality of YHWH. If YHWH is central, the servant (Obed) of YHWH can come from any nation through covenant.

Theological Analysis

Genealogy informs identity. This means that a genealogy in Scripture also functions as a theology of identity that addresses this dilemma: what happens when someone who is central to Israel's identity, the person with whom God made a divine covenant, is found to have foreign blood? The answer in Ruth allows for the foreigner to be adopted, married, or otherwise assimilated into the family. Ruth marries into the family of Israel and her great-grandson David is adopted into YHWH's family (through the Davidic Covenant in 2 Sam 7). In both instances, the outsider or other becomes family by a willing commitment, an act of *hesed*/faithfulness, which creates family where there was none before. Thus Ruth is a commentary itself on genealogy. It does more than offer a historical and political tie to the past and future; it offers an alternate understanding of history. Ruth reminds us that our stories, our very histories, are dialogic, that is, their meanings are enhanced when we include all the elements and traditions. One purpose of a genealogy is to prove one's pedigree. This would most certainly be the case for a king. The presence of covenant between Naomi and Ruth and subsequently between Boaz and Ruth introduces the theological truth that covenant is the determining factor in one's family or pedigree.

Whether Ruth initiates a dialogue with Ezra–Nehemiah or with the people during the ninth century BCE, it offers a countertradition to a culture where identity is so closely tied to family/clan, kinship group/tribe, and land. Ruth offers to those who question David's legitimacy because of his Moabite ancestry not an apology, but an alternate reality. The genealogy legitimizes Ruth, and by extension David. To the Ezra–Nehemiah community that focuses on racial/ethnic, and ultimately religious purity as the litmus test for being one of God's chosen, the story of Ruth is a subversive/anti-genealogy.

Unlike an oral genealogy that can be adjusted to fit the context or serve the function of the storyteller, the written genealogy's ability to be altered is "severely limited" (Wilson 1977, 55). What then happens when an oral genealogy is written down? In the case of Ruth, it appears that the genealogy has enjoyed a number of dialogue partners that have allowed it to maintain some characteristics of an oral genealogy. Ruth talks back to the assumptions that would have been held by the community of Israel around the time of David's rule and it would have offered an alternative to the assumptions held by the Ezra–Nehemiah community. It offers a countertradition that is not easily ignored. To the ninth-century audience, Ruth presents a contradiction. If David is God's anointed and his great-grandmother is a Moabite, something has to give. Either David has to stop being God's anointed or Ruth has to be incorporated back into Israel. If Ruth is written during the time of Ezra–Nehemiah, the narrative reminds a community focused on "purity" that its most beloved king had a Moabite great-grandmother. Ruth offers a theological vision where the faithfulness of God is not limited to land or people, or even to Israel's understanding of God's ordinances.

In Ruth, women's decisions precede those of men. In this book, Ruth's decision in chapter 1 is the central action, the moment that changes the course of events. The formal and public exchange between Boaz and his unnamed relative is a manifestation of the private exchange between Naomi and Ruth in no-man's-land between Moab and Bethlehem. Similarly, the plan of Naomi and Ruth to glean grain and subsequently a husband is made in private but made manifest later on in the narrative.

This reminds us that God's *hesed,* or faithfulness, by definition crosses boundaries in its desire to be in relationship with God's creation. Thus the faithfulness of Ruth crosses the boundaries of land in chapter 1, family in chapter 2, propriety in chapter 3, and history in chapter 4. In each of these cases, the boundary is crossed with words that are followed by action. In chapter 1, Ruth makes a vow that is performative speech. In so doing she forms a new bond with Naomi. In chapter 2, Boaz speaks to Ruth the Moabite and calls her "my daughter." Boaz's address to Ruth

changes the rubrics of identity. Instead of allowing her to be identified and known by the characteristics of her culture's reputation
or characteristics, Boaz's words offer a different way of relating to
the outsider—making them family. This act of making an outsider
family is what is accomplished through the act of marriage. In
chapter 3, Ruth crosses the boundaries of propriety, risking safety
and reputation to secure the family that she and Naomi need for
survival.

If Ruth is offering a countertradition to the one that ties identity to land and people, is the book successful in subverting the
tradition? After all, Ruth the Moabite ends up as the wife of a
prominent man who belongs to a well-known family, in the line
of Judah. She now has all the identity markers the narrative
started with. Is the point of this story simply to absorb outsiders
into Israel or is it to redefine what it means to belong to the
nation of Israel? How does Ruth challenge the status quo from
inside?

The interpretation of Ruth as absorbed into the family of Boaz
is dependent in part upon a reading that views the marriage and
genealogy as the climax of the narrative. This would be expected
since the narrative does in fact have a comedic structure. Within
the existing structure, however, the opening decisive moment
changes everything. Ruth may be incorporated into an upstand-
ing family, but her presence, her Moabite blood, and her *hesed*
transform from the inside. Ruth's incorporation into the family
entails a redefinition of family. When the outsiders become the
insiders, the family is irrevocably altered. The genealogy at the
end shows us that the transformation started with performative
speech in chapter 1, but it had a ripple effect that extended all the
way to the beloved king David. As is the case with the faithfulness
of God, the Ruth narrative demonstrates that *hesed* is pervasive.

A dialogue between the genealogy at the end of chapter 4 and
Ruth's vow in chapter 1 suggests that the presence of the Moabite
and her determination to demonstrate *hesed* results not in just
another genealogy at the end, but in a genealogy that demands a
prolonged narrative explanation. Is the genealogy an appendix to
the narrative, or is the narrative an explication or preface to the

genealogy—a way of explaining how such a genealogy came to be? In other words, to what extent does the story of Ruth provide an accompanying "oral" tradition to a preexisting genealogy? The narrative is what allows the genealogy to have application to a variety of times and settings. The story, with its unique historical placement (during the time of the judges), allows for dialogue with a community that attempts to find its identity out of a mixed multitude, whether that be a postexilic community that finds its people intermarried or the community of the ninth century BCE who struggles with the "mixed blood" of their most beloved king.

CONCLUSION

Ruth is a story about survival. As such, it can function for subsequent audiences as a survival manual disguised as a comedy. A comedy usually begins with a normal society, into which some crisis comes, upsetting the norms and creating conflict. The disruption can be natural or supernatural, but the structure of the comedy will move to resolve the conflict and reestablish a society. Often the society at the end of the comedy is transformed; it sometimes incorporates elements or results of the chaos into the new order. In other words, the "happily ever after" at the end of a comedy is not the "once upon a time" with which the story began. The resolution in a comedy comes in part from a reintegration of people into the group and a recommitment to a shared life together. This often involves compromise and the acceptance of some limitations within a given culture. The crisis of a comedy is one that threatens identity within a society and the resolution of the crisis is some form of reintegration. The comedy may focus on a few individuals, but the individual is envisioned in relationship with a community.

Scholars often distinguish between comedic and tragic structure by describing the comedy as "U" in shape, while the tragedy is an inverted "U." The former begins in order, descends into a crisis, and then the crisis is resolved. The tragedy begins with the crisis, which is initially addressed by the hero. Unfortunately, the hero's tragic flaw results in another crisis that is only resolved with the hero's death.

This simple description of the comedic and tragic structures highlights the similarities between the two. Both comedy and tragedy involve conflict and resolution. A comedy has tragic elements and often a tragedy contains the comedic. The difference between the two has to do with where the story begins and ends, and how the conflict is resolved. A tragic figure often stands apart from or in opposition to the community and attempts to deal with the conflict alone. Tragic heroes tend not to compromise with a society's value system. For this reason the conflict in a tragedy is resolved with the tragic figure's death. A tragedy ends looking back while the end of a comedy anticipates a future.

In the story of Ruth, Naomi interjects the tragic element. In 1:8-13, she stands at the crossroads with her daughters-in-law, and explains to them that they must leave her because she has nothing to offer—her life is essentially over. Like a tragic hero, her speech contains multiple references to herself. When she returns home at the conclusion of chapter 1 (v. 20) she tells the women to call her Mara, a name that reflects her desolation. On neither of these occasions is Naomi alone. When she gives the first speech, she is with her daughters-in-law, whom she is trying to send away. In the second, Ruth is standing beside her. In between Naomi's two speeches about her dismal situation is Ruth's vow of fidelity. In the midst of Naomi's tragic moments, Ruth makes a commitment to family/community that alters Naomi's course bent on tragedy. Ruth affirms what we understand about comedy and tragedy. A character's response to crisis may determine whether their story will be a tragedy or a comedy. The survival manual of Ruth teaches us that tragic events can be transformed into a comedic ending.

A comedy affirms our desire for family and community. Unlike a tragic hero, Ruth bends to the norms of another society out of a commitment to Naomi as her family. Ruth's decision to cling to Naomi is a decision that places the concerns of the community over the concerns of an individual, and the crisis in Naomi's family is eventually resolved as a result. The widowed Israelite and the widowed Moabitess are reintegrated into a society that is transformed by their presence.

The story of Ruth begins and ends with family, the building

block of this society. The family of Boaz, Naomi, Mahlon, and Chilion is decimated by famine, displacement, and death. The faithfulness of Ruth the Moabite and, subsequently, that of Boaz allow for the redemption of the deceased Elimelech. The "name" of the deceased is preserved through progeny, land, and blessing. The tripartite understanding of "name" as it connotes identity also evokes the promise made to Abraham. The ancestor was promised land, descendants, and blessing, and, in addition, God promised to make his "name great" so that he would be a blessing. It is no coincidence that the elements of the blessing of Abraham are core elements of identity among the children of Israel.

Central to this construct of identity is the act of being set apart. After all, Abraham's call is a call to leave behind father and land for another land that God will show him. To some extent, this call away from others has been preserved in Israel in the practice of endogamy, the practice of marrying inside one's community or people. The exclusion of others, namely foreign wives, meant that the practices of family and clan were preserved. But our traditions of Abraham's call must include the fact that he left his father, but not his wife or his nephew. His forsaking of his family was, effectively, a leaving behind of one family order for another, forming a different family with YHWH.

Ruth's decision to cling to Naomi presents the reader with a challenge. Will we read this story as that of a Moabite, an outsider, or foreign woman? Or will we read it as the story of someone who, like Abraham, left behind her family and land for another land, namely that of her widowed and childless mother-in-law? If we read the story on analogy with that of Abraham, Ruth is not a despised outsider but a revered ancestress. The lens through which we read the narrative determines, among other things, Ruth's identity.

Using identity as an interpretive lens, we began with the premise that identity, the set of characteristics that allow a person to be known and identified within a group, is a construct that serves the purposes of a specific culture at a specific time. In Israel, the construct of identity serves a religious and national purpose. The religious purpose is to distinguish between the people of YHWH and everyone else. Israel is, after all, a people called out from others and thus its identity is shaped by an awareness of other cultures. As a nation, Israel enters a land that is populated and must constantly define itself over and against the others, be they Perizzite, Jebusite, Moabite, Ammonite, and so on.

For a people who come onto the existing scene of Canaan, whatever that may have been, its sense of self and its sense of survival depend on a religious and political separation from the other. If Israel assimilates the religious practices of her neighbors, she would cease to exist as a people. Central to Israel's identity is an understanding of herself as distinct from the people who surround her, and this distinctiveness centers on her worship and devotion to YHWH, who makes specific demands on the people that are expressed through the covenant. The worship of God is supported by the prohibition against intermarriage. Scripture tends to talk about foreign marriage as marriage to foreign women. This may make sense if we remember that men (or parents) choose wives, and not the other way around. It has also been argued that women or mothers have tremendous influence on the religious practices and beliefs in the home. The result is that by using the term "foreign women" to describe intermarriage, infidelity to God's covenant in this regard becomes engendered. The foreign woman becomes the icon of inappropriate influences.

Israel's explanation for the destruction of the Northern Kingdom by Assyria in 721 BCE and the exile of the Southern Kingdom in 587 BCE was a theological one. Israel was removed from the land of promise because she continually broke the covenant. The covenant is the binding agreement that bound Israel to God. It is the covenant that made these people kin or family with God and they were bound through faithfulness to God just as a groom and bride make a covenant that binds them together. Israel broke the covenant when she worshiped the other gods of its neighbors. The act of Israel's worship of other gods is described in Scripture as an act of infidelity in a marriage. God was in covenant with a people who were incapable of faithfulness, a wife who "whored after" other gods (Ezek16:26-29).

In psychological terms, this construction of "other" is called encoding (pp. 61-62). When the eyes rest on a person, the brain quickly researches its records to determine whether the individual is known or unknown. The brain will send a message back identifying the individual as familiar or unknown—sometimes the eyes encounter a familiar face in an unknown context and this results in a disconnect. That is how we distinguish between the familiar and the strange. But this process of file keeping is not neutral. We have values that are assigned to the images on file. It is the reason that we often have a visceral response to others based on appearance; we associate certain characteristics with certain images. For example, many action films in the early 1990s cast Arab-looking actors as the bad guys. The casting was based on a cultural association that became affirmed through repetition.

In addition to the individual cognitive process of recognition and memory, communities have a collective series of images of individuals or others. In Scripture we observe the encoding of the Moabite as other. Genesis 19 and Deut 23:3 are passages that contribute to a memory of Moab and the Moabites. Each passage functions like an image in the brain. Each passage encodes the corporate memory of the people of Israel so that the mention of the word "Moabite" brings to mind disgust, distrust, or disdain. For this reason, early audiences of the story of Ruth were not neutral about the Moabites. The story of Ruth's faithfulness offers an alternative image of the Moabite women. This image now is added to the catalog of images in the community's collective memory. The new image, like a disaster in a comedy or a tragedy, causes conflict. How will the community respond to this image that disrupts a traditional understanding of this other? In Ruth, the choice is not left to Israel (Naomi). Rather, Ruth takes the initiative and binds herself to Naomi with a vow that invokes YHWH.

For the narrator of Ruth, sending away the foreign wife is no more easily accomplished than removing David's great-grandmother from his bloodline. Here the narrative looks backward (like a tragedy) and forward (like a comedy), claiming that the "other" was a part of the family long ago. Therefore, Israel's future identity depends on a sense of family that recognizes the other as family and not as alien. In the same way that Abraham's call is both a call from known family to new family, Israel's future will depend on an identity that lives in tension with being unique and inclusive. Is Israel's uniqueness found in her ability to "encode" or "assimilate" the other into the family, thereby constantly creating new understandings of family?

If Ruth's Earliest Audiences Heard Ruth During the Ninth Century BCE

David laid claim to the throne on the basis of his call by God, demonstrated through his anointment. David was the messiah, or anointed one. Like Saul, his call came from God and through the prophet, and it stood to reason that like Saul, the length and terms of his reign were subject to God's wishes (before the Davidic covenant). Those who would have opposed David or maintained loyalty to the house of Saul could have raised David's Moabite ancestry as an obstacle to David's reign. Clearly, the descendant of a Moabite could not sit on the throne as the Moabites were "other" in their ethnicity and worship. Moreover, they were named by God as people to be avoided (tenth generation) because of their inhospitality to Israel. Such a strong prohibition against the Moabites would make it seemingly impossible for the messiah to have Moabite ancestry. For this audience, the story of Ruth would promote the faithfulness of Ruth, perhaps to depict her as an "exceptional" other—one who, because of her extraordinary devotion to YHWH, is cast in the role of proselyte.

With the Davidic covenant and the introduction of dynastic succession ordained by God come questions of the legitimacy of David's line. To this audience, the language of adoption expressed through the use of the term "my daughter" by both Naomi and Boaz would have supported the use of parent/child language in the adoption imagery of the Davidic covenant. YHWH makes a covenant with David and the covenant is performative speech that makes it so, just as Ruth's vow/covenant to Naomi makes them family. Ultimately, the covenant overrides any other claims on one's identity.

If Ruth's Earliest Audiences Heard Ruth During the Return to the Land

Israel's return to the land after exile is laden with questions around identity. If, prior to the exile, Israel's identity was tied to her notion of belonging to God through covenant and being in the land of promise, how does one go about the business of reconstructing an identity when the markers previously used are gone? What are the terms of the covenant now, when one considers that the experience of the exile has shaped the people of Israel? Moreover, if we place the writing of Ruth to the time of the exile, how does a people establish itself in a barren land (a metaphorical famine) without a temple or an infrastructure? When kinship groups and tribal boundaries have been ignored for years in the homeland, and those returning from the Diaspora have intermarried, how does one begin the work of rebuilding a nation? Who, then, under these circumstances is Israel?

Often, individuals separated from their markers of identity seize upon whatever remnants are available. Ezra offers a narrative of Israel's return. The postexilic period is its setting (the sixth and fifth centuries BCE), and the rebuilding of the city's boundary wall and Temple is its theme. Embedded in all this construction is the reconstruction of a national identity. Ezra 9:1-16 recounts the denunciation of marriages to foreign women, and the sending away of these wives and children. The names of the men who sent their wives away were listed, but the text of Ezra ends there—with no word on what happens to the many wives and even more children. Where did they go and who provided for them? The fervor of the narrative is focused on the identity of Israel as a pure race, which has contaminated itself: "Thus the holy seed has mixed itself with the peoples of the lands" (Ezra 9:2). Certainly the fervor to be "pure" as a people would have been a clearly identifiable demonstration of fidelity to YHWH, an expression of devotion and a desire to be set apart once again.

Ruth in this context makes a very strong case against this sense of identity based on racial purity. It serves to remind the people of another tradition that is central to their identity. This countertradition reminds Israel that her identity is rooted in covenant, a contractual bond of faithfulness that creates family out of disparate elements. It is on the basis of covenant that Israel is God's people.

Ruth in Matthew 1

The first chapter of Matthew, the first book in the New Testament, contains a genealogy of Jesus that is unique in that it mentions Tamar, Rahab, Ruth, and the wife of Uriah in addition to Mary, mother of Jesus. The mention of women in a genealogy is rare. Moreover, the mention of these particular women causes the reader to ask, what is Matthew trying to do? If Matthew is writing to a Jewish audience, then we would expect his genealogy to prove pedigree. There are elements of Matthew's genealogy that suggest this is his intention. He begins with Abraham, and covers fourteen generations to David and goes through the next fourteen generations to the exile, and then follows the next fourteen generations that lead to Jesus, the messiah. The three sets of fourteen generations implies that it is time for the messiah. Although the genealogy does not mention every ancestor, it carefully chooses those whose names would make a strong case for Jesus as the messiah, which makes the mention of these women all the more curious, until we place Matt 1 in dialogue with Ruth 4:18-22.

The dialogue between Ruth's genealogy and Matthew's genealogy suggests that Matthew uses the genre/form of the genealogy because that would be expected, while simultaneously offering a critique on the cultural constructs that place limits on the work of God. Matthew's listing of these women is a countertradition embedded in a traditional genealogy. It serves the purpose of reminding his readers that they have a history of God working in unconventional ways. Moreover, the genealogy affirms that some of Israel's greatest moments come from individuals' unusual encounters with God in unlikely places.

A Contemporary Reading of Ruth: Ethnicity and Race

In colonial America, race took on a unique shape as the evolving institution of slavery demanded that a distinction be made between the African captives and their captors. Hence, the constructs of white and black replaced specific national identity. Somalis, Ghanaians, Liberians, and Nigerians, from Ibo or Igbo and other tribes, became "black" or "African," and the Spanish, Dutch, Portuguese, French, English, Italian, and German population became "white." The construct served the purpose of delineating between two classes of beings in a society where the economic system depended on them remaining separate. This separation along the lines of race came when the division between slave and master along religious lines proved ineffective. In spite of the carefully constructed divisions there were and there are moments when the lines between insider and outsider have been hard to maintain. In the time of slavery, the divide between black and white required a carefully constructed system for people of mixed race, producing the terms mulatto, quadroon, octoroon, and septaroon. If someone is of mixed blood, where do they fit in society? The rules in some southern states ruled one drop of black blood made a person black. This allowed for slaves fathered by their masters to remain slaves. It also supported the notion that people of African descent were less human than their European counterparts.

One crack in the system was that mixed-race people with a certain set of features could "pass" for white if they were able to get to a place where no one knew them or their families. In this instance, appearance was the primary basis upon which one was recognized as black or white. If a mixed-race person had the right look, access to the right social conventions, and the right amount of education, he or she could be virtually white.

In contemporary times we observe another challenge to this racial construct in the refusal of mixed-race people to choose one category over another, insisting that they are both or many things. Their status in our society points to the complexities of race that never went away. It reminds us that the line between insiders and outsiders has never been a firm one.

Although the "one-drop" rule is no longer in effect, it should not be lost on us that the first black president of the United States is, in fact, biracial. Of Kenyan and Anglo-American descent,

Barack Obama is African American in the most literal sense of the term. But he is considered by most to be African American because in our country there is still the vestige of slavery in the construct of American identity that uses the categories of black and white.

It is of interest that Ruth moves beyond the confines of society by embracing the religion of the other. When Ruth invokes the covenant form in a strange place, and under strange circumstances, she is transforming the practice itself, stretching the metaphor of covenant, because she has an understanding of *hesed*/faithfulness that is not limited by a cultural construct.

In breaking out of the confines that limit her own identity, Ruth makes evident the extent to which the other characters in the narrative are limited by this construct as well. Naomi's gender and state of widowhood leave her "bereft," in spite of the faithful daughter-in-law in chapter 1. At the conclusion of the story, the women are able to proclaim that Naomi's daughter-in-law is better to her than seven sons. Boaz too, we discover, is limited by his age. As an older man, he perceives himself as someone who is not deserving of the devotion and promise of new life that Ruth represents. Again, Ruth's *hesed*/faithfulness reminds us that YHWH does not recognize the constraints of a society.

A Contemporary Reading of Ruth: Gender

In contemporary American culture, terms like "post-racial" and "post-gender" have been used to describe a perceived development in society that places us beyond the constraints of race, gender, and sexual orientation. In the "post-_____" dialogue I am interested in the following: first, on what basis do we determine that the walls that divide us have been torn down? And second, does the "post-_____" world require that our distinctive characteristics go away? This is the concern on the part of some feminist scholars about the end of Ruth. The powerful and assertive heroine of chapter 1 is silent in chapter 4 where she is assimilated into the house of Israel and her child is placed on the bosom of her mother-in-law, Naomi.

CONCLUSION

In order to address the concerns around Ruth's assimilation and subsequent disappearance, one must return to the question of how one forms a construct of identity. What does it mean for Ruth to "count" in her cultural contexts and what would be required of contemporary readers? For the ANE cultural context, one's identity is rooted in familial constructs and land. This context holds during the monarchy. In fact, it is this construct of identity that could call David's ancestry into question. The assembly of people who return for the purpose of rebuilding the land struggles to create an identity construct. The earlier construct presents challenges that result from people's separation from the land and the practice of intermarriage. In some ways, Ruth's challenge to the norms of a given society provides an opportunity to engage in a dialogue about how one is selected as an insider or an outsider. In Ruth, faithfulness/*hesed* opens up possibilities between people that did not previously exist, in much the same way God's faithfulness/*hesed* to Israel allowed for a covenant that would not have existed otherwise. Moreover, it was God's *hesed* that allowed for Israel to have new beginnings after failing to keep the covenant.

The concern that Ruth is absorbed in the narrative comes from another construct of identity. This construct values individual autonomy. Ruth's appeal to many readers comes from her choice in chapter 1 to stay with Naomi in spite of Naomi's urging, which some interpret as an independent act. Also, Ruth's initiative in chapter 2 to procure food is seen as the behavior of someone acting as an individual.

A dialogic reading that takes other cultural constructs into account introduces the possibility that Ruth's behavior in chapters 1 and 2 is not an expression of individualism but one of service to the family. If that is the case, it could be argued that Ruth's ultimate goal was to be assimilated and absorbed into this Israelite family.

This raises the question of the extent to which we can distinguish between the concerns of the reader and that of text. Moreover, we must consider the extent to which concerns about Ruth are appropriate. Is she in this narrative an individual or a literary construct? As a character in the story, Ruth serves a function. She plays a role in a dialogic comedy that has theological implications. In a story about redemption, the needs of the community—that is, the preservation of the family—trump the needs of the individual. This is the case not only for Ruth, but for Boaz as well. The person who demonstrates *hesed*/faithfulness is characteristically one who sacrifices for the well-being of others. The challenge this depiction of faithfulness presents to some modern readers is the history of women who have been forced into positions of faithfulness. How does one appropriate this vision of God's faithfulness in narrative when it carries a history of assigned roles for modern women?

One might ask at the end of the book the same question asked at the beginning. Why is the name of this book "Ruth" and not "Naomi"? The fact that the tradition remembers this story under the name of the Moabite is no small matter. Here the construct of identity as it exists in the ancient Near East is useful. It is the remembering of the ancestor that keeps the deceased alive. Thus, it is Ruth who is remembered and named. The Moabite does not disappear; rather, she is the reference point for the reader to enter into the genealogy, the official or unofficial record of the line of Judah. She is named as one of the five women in Matthew's genealogy of Jesus, along with Tamar, Rahab, Bathsheba, and Mary.

It is the Moabite who demonstrates the faithfulness of God that is not limited by location, famine, plenty, ethnicity, or even sense. Her steadfast presence is what sustains a people on the brink of extinction. It is this faithfulness that speaks to Israel again and again throughout her history—both when she struggles to understand herself as a nation and when she struggles to define herself after the exile. It is the faithfulness of God that is Israel's point of orientation. It is in God's *hesed* that we find our origins and it is to the faithfulness of this God that we return.

SELECT BIBLIOGRAPHY

Aranov, Maurice Moshe. 1977. *The Biblical Threshing-Floor in the Light of the Ancient Near Eastern Evidence: Evolution of an Institution.* Ann Arbor, Mich.: University Microfilms International.

Austin, J. L. 1962. *How to Do Things with Words.* Cambridge, Mass.: Harvard University Press.

Bailey, Randall. 1995. "They're Nothing but Incestuous Bastards: The Polemical Use of Sex and Sexuality in Hebrew Canon Narratives," in *Social Location and Biblical Interpretation in the United States.* Vol. 1 of *Reading from This Place.* Edited by Fernando F. Segovia and Mary Ann Tolbert. Minneapolis: Fortress.

Bakhtin, M. M. 1981. *The Dialogic Imagination: Four Essays by M. M. Bakhtin.* Austin: University of Texas Press.

Berlin, Adele. 1989. *Notes on Ruth in The Harper Collins Study Bible.* Edited by Wayne A. Meeks. New York: Harper Collins.

Brown, Francis, S. R. Driver, and Charles Briggs. 2001. *The Brown-Driver-Briggs Hebrew and English Lexicon.* Peabody, Mass.: Hendrickson.

Campbell, Edward F. 1975. *Ruth.* The Anchor Bible. New York: Doubleday.

Cazelles, Henri. 1992. "Bethlehem." Pages 712-15 in vol. 1 of *The Anchor Bible Dictionary.* New York: Doubleday.

Coogan, David M. 2006. *The Old Testament: A Historical and Literary Introduction to the Hebrew Scriptures.* New York: Oxford University Press.

Cook, Stephen. 2009. "Death, Kinship and Community: Afterlife and the *hesed* Ideal in Israel." Pages 106-121 in *The Family in Life and in Death: The Family in Ancient Israel.* Edited by Patricia Dutcher-Walls. New York: T & T Clark.

Davis, Ellen, and Margaret Adam Parker. 2003. *Who Are You, My Daughter?* Louisville: Westminster John Knox.

Dube, Muse, ed. 2001. *Other Ways of Reading: African Women and the Bible.* Atlanta: Society of Biblical Literature.

Dunker, *Westoslichen Divan,* Dunker's ed. of Goethe's *Werke,* p. 217, as cited by Louis B. Wolfenson in "The Character, Contents and Date of Ruth," in *The American Journal of Semitic Languages and Literatures,* Volume XXVII, number 4, 1911.

Farmer, Kathleen. 2003. "Ruth." Pages 383-84 in *The New Interpreters Study Bible.* Edited by Walter J. Harrelson. Nashville: Abingdon Press.

Fisch, Harold. 1982. "Ruth and the Structure of Covenant History," *Vetus Testamentum* 32:425-37.

Fontaine, Carol. 2000. "Lilith." Page 531 in *Women in Scripture.* Edited by Carol Meyers. New York: Houghton Mifflin.

Frye, Northrop. 1957. *Anatomy of Criticism: Four Essays.* Princeton, N.J.: Princeton University Press.

Gafney, Wil. 2009. "Ruth." Pages 249-54 in *The Africana Bible.* Edited by Hugh Paige. Minneapolis: Fortress.

Ginzberg, Louis. 1956. *Legends of the Bible.* Philadelphia: The Jewish Publication Society.

The Harper Collins Study Bible, Student Edition, Harold Attridge, General Editor, Revised Edition, Wayne A. Meeks, General Editor, Original Edition, 2006. New York: Harper Collins Publishers

Hendel, Ronald, Chana Kronfeld and Ilana Pardes. 2010 "Gender and Sexuality" in R*eading Genesis: Ten Methods.* Edited by Ronald Hendel. New York: Cambridge University Press.

———. Notes on Genesis in the *Harper Collins Study Bible, Student Edition,* Harold Attridge, General Editor, 2006. New York: Harper Collins Publishers.

Johnston, Ian. "Dramatic Structure: Comedy and Tragedy" (lecture, Malaspina University College, British Columbia).

King, Philip J., and Lawrence E. Stager. 2001. *Life in Biblical Israel*. Library of Ancient Israel. Louisville: Westminster John Knox.

LaCocque, Andre. 1990. *The Feminine Unconventional*. Minneapolis: Fortress.

———. 2004. *Ruth*. A Continental Commentary. Minneapolis: Fortress.

Levenson, Jon. 1985. *Sinai and Zion*. San Francisco: Harper San Francisco.

Levine, A. J. 1992. "Ruth." Pages 78-84 in *The Women's Bible Commentary*. Edited by Carol Newsom and Sharon Ringe. Louisville: Westminster John Knox.

Morson, Gary Saul, and Caryl Emerson. 1990. *Mikhail Bakhtin: Creation of a Prosaics*. Stanford, Calif.: Stanford University Press.

Nielsen, Kirsten. 1997. *Ruth*. The Old Testament Library. Louisville: Westminster John Knox.

Pardes, Ilana. 1992. *Countertraditions in the Bible: A Feminist Approach*. Cambridge, Mass.: Harvard University Press.

Polzin, Robert. 1989. *Samuel and the Deuteronomist: A Literary Study of the Deuteronomic History*. Bloomington & Indianapolis: Indiana University Press.

Robertson, Warren C. 2010. *Drought, Famine, Plague and Pestilence: Ancient Israel's Understanding of and Responses to Natural Catastrophes*. Piscataway, N.J.: Gorgias.

Sakenfeld, Katharine Doob. 1989. *Ruth. Interpretation: A Bible Commentary for Teaching and Preaching*. Louisville: John Knox.

———. 2003. *Just Wives? Stories of Power and Survival in the Old Testament and Today*. Louisville: Westminster John Knox.

Sasson, Jacques. 1979. *Ruth: A New Translation with a Philological Commentary and a Formalist-Folklorist Interpretation*. Baltimore: The Johns Hopkins University Press.

Streete, Gail Corrington. 1997. *The Strange Woman: Power and Sex in the Bible*. Louisville: John Knox.

Trible, Phyllis. 1982. "A Human Comedy: The Book of Ruth." Pages 161–90 in *Literary Interpretations of Biblical Narratives*.

Edited by Kenneth R. R. Gros Louis. Nashville: Abingdon Press.

Tull, Patricia. 2003. *Esther and Ruth*. Louisville: Westminster John Knox.

Weems, Renita J. 1988. *Just a Sister Away: A Womanist Vision of Women's Relationships in the Bible*. San Diego: LuraMedia.

Wilson, Robert R. 1977. *Genealogy and History in the Biblical World. Yale Near Eastern Researchers*. New Haven: Yale University Press.

SUBJECT INDEX